WHAT HAPPENED TO CIVILITY

What Happened to

CIVILITY

THE PROMISE AND FAILURE OF
MONTAIGNE'S MODERN PROJECT

ANN HARTLE

University of Notre Dame Press
Notre Dame, Indiana

Published by the University of Notre Dame Press
Notre Dame, Indiana 46556
undpress.nd.edu

Published in the United States of America

Library of Congress Control Number: 2021948628

ISBN: 978-0-268-20232-3 (Hardback)
ISBN: 978-0-268-20233-0 (Paperback)
ISBN: 978-0-268-20234-7 (WebPDF)
ISBN: 978-0-268-20231-6 (Epub)

For Robert and Shannon

CONTENTS

ACKNOWLEDGMENTS

I wish to express my gratitude to Francis Slade, whose understanding of the origins of modern philosophy has shaped my own views and whose work is foundational for this book. My thanks are due to John Kekes, who read an earlier version of this book and gave me many very helpful suggestions. The two reviewers for the press helped me to clarify and sharpen my argument. Margaret Matthews assisted me with the research on Montaigne. I am grateful for that assistance as well as additional forms of support funded by the Heilbrun Distinguished Emeritus Fellowship through the Emory University Emeritus College. An NEH Fundamental Questions grant funded a freshman seminar on civility that I designed and taught in 2014. The seminar was the occasion for developing my interest in this topic.

INTRODUCTION

The human condition in our postmodern, post-Christian, Western world is a condition of both unprecedented individual freedom and deep cultural division. The freedom of the self-creating individual from nature and from tradition extends even to the choice of one's gender, while the norms of individual choice are so radically opposed that it is no longer possible to speak to each other in the terms of a common culture. Instead of having a common culture grounded in a shared tradition, we are increasingly divided between two cultures at war with each other: a culture of those who regard themselves as elite "self-creating" individuals not bound by the norms of tradition and the culture of those who do regard themselves as bound by traditional norms, which they believe society should foster. Civility is supposed to be the bond that holds us together in peace and mutual respect. However, with the deepening of cultural differences, civility has deteriorated alarmingly.

My purpose is to gain clarity about our present condition and to understand how we arrived at this point where civility seems impossible. What is civility and why has it disappeared?

The idea of civility has a long history going back as far as ancient Rome, and it admits of a wide range of meanings from simple courtesy to what it means to be "civilized" in terms of education in the entire culture of a civilization. Civility, as I discuss it here, is the social bond that makes it possible for individuals to live in peace in the political and social structures of the modern Western world. When we say today that civility has failed, I take it that that is what we mean by civility.

Civility, of course, cannot account for every aspect of human life in the modern world. Ideas such as human rights, sovereignty, representative government, and the general will have all shaped the structures of our political life. Civility as I present it here and as I believe Montaigne understood it pertains specifically to *social* interactions. Society (as I discuss it in chapter 2) is the counterpart of the modern state: a society can be *civil* to the extent that it is free of the coercive power of the state. Civility is the character that is indispensable for individuals to live in and enjoy the human interactions of a free society.

Civility, then, is not simply good manners and courtesy. It is a complete moral character, including many qualities that we think of today as "virtues" but that, although they were present to one degree or another, were not considered virtues in the premodern world. These qualities or dispositions are promise keeping, generosity, compassion, forgiveness, trust, toleration, openness, sincerity, self-disclosure, and similar qualities that might be called "social virtues." Civility is supposed to replace the traditional moral virtues as the social bond. When we say that civility has failed, we mean that these qualities are in danger of disappearing and that the social bond is disintegrating.

How and when does this modern notion of civility come on the scene? As Teresa Bejan demonstrates, this concept of civility arose "in early modern attempts to refasten the social bonds severed by the Reformation."[1] The Reformation destroyed the unity of Christendom, rejecting the authority of tradition in favor of the authority of Scripture alone. At that point, civility comes into existence to replace the tradition as the social bond.

According to Michael Oakeshott, early modern European history was a moment when the civil character became visible and received its classic expression in the *Essays* of Montaigne.[2] To say that Montaigne "invented" civility is to say that he saw, in the ruins of the tradition, the possibility of a new social bond and that he formed the new civil character out of the fragments of the tradition. He uses historical examples and fragments of ancient philosophy to give expression, in familiar terms, to the new order that he brings into being. He puts the past into the service of his own new philosophical project.

Montaigne constructs this civil character out of the fragments of the shattered classical-Christian tradition—in particular, from classical magnanimity and Christian charity. Montaigne often presents himself as a "third" type, a transformation of and alternative to both classical and Christian types. For example, as Pierre Manent argues, Montaigne transforms classical magnanimity by renouncing honor, and he transforms Christian humility by confessing not his sins but his mere human weakness.[3] And, as I attempt to show, the centrality of compassion in modern moral discourse has its source in Christian charity.

To say that civility is a *philosophical* invention does not mean that only the philosopher can be civil or that all must become philosophers in order to be civil. Rather, Montaigne displays this character in the *Essays* as a new possibility for human being. My claim is that the *Essays* are the first act of self-conscious civility. Philosophy, as he engages in it, makes his civility self-conscious. But for most people, civility is not, cannot, and should not be self-conscious in this philosophical sense, because true reformation must take place at the level of unreflective mores and pre-reflective sensibilities.

The *Essays* are addressed not only to philosophers but to "the great," to the gentlemen of his day who are ready to break with the old standards of nobility. Montaigne writes in order to reform the *mores* of his culture, a reformation for which he must have thought the culture was prepared. He does not present philosophical arguments to persuade his readers to reform themselves: that is why the *Essays* do not look like philosophy. Rather, he presents himself as an example or type of a new moral character, and the success of the *Essays* shows that this character was indeed an attractive possibility to his contemporaries. As David Quint argues in *Montaigne and the Quality of Mercy*,[4] Montaigne's intention is the transformation of the mores of the nobility through the replacement of valor by mercy and compassion as the standard of noble action. The revaluations that occur throughout the *Essays*, especially his preference for the easy over the difficult, point to a "softening" of morals that Montaigne refers to as the "ease" of virtue. Montaigne's reformation might be described as the replacement of the traditional moral virtues by the qualities of civility.

In the contrasts that I make between the old order of the tradition and the new, modern moral and political order, I do not intend to suggest that the premodern world was a world of perfect moral virtue and peaceful harmony. The ancient city was the scene of frequent revolutions resulting from the competition to rule among the various factions. And in Montaigne's lifetime, France was torn apart by civil and religious wars. Modern political philosophers, including Montaigne, are concerned to address the imperfections of both ancient and medieval political arrangements.

I do want to claim, however, that the failure of civility that we experience today reveals just what has been lost in the movement from sacred tradition as the social bond to modern forms of moral and political life. What has been lost is the public standard of moral virtue, the cultural constraints of honor and shame, and the possibility of moral community.

The argument of my book is that civility is a human, philosophical invention and that civility fails because it is a human, philosophical invention. Civility breaks under the pressure of an extreme tension. That is, civility is supposed to make possible the social space in which the individual is free to pursue the good in his own way, to make himself to be what he wants to be, freeing him from the norms of the tradition. This freedom comes from doing away with the orientation to the divine that is essential to the tradition. However, civility, as Montaigne presents it, is constructed out of the fragments of the shattered tradition—in particular, from classical magnanimity and Christian charity, but now reordered from the divine to man as man. Civility fails because those fragments, cut off from the whole of the tradition that gives them life and in which they have their true meaning, wither and die. Magnanimity, reduced to generosity and cut off from the honor due to noble deeds, loses all public recognition and disappears. Charity, reduced to compassion and cut off from the mystery of salvation, becomes distorted and perverted.

The failure of civility reveals this tension at the heart of civility: civility replaces the tradition as the social bond and makes possible the conditions for free, self-creating individuals to live in peace together, but at the same time, civility needs the tradition to keep alive the qualities of nobility and charity from which it is created. In other words, civility is built on the ruins of the very tradition that alone can give it life. The failure of civility is the moral disaster that shows us what civility requires. Civility alone is not sufficient to constitute the social bond: it must have the continuing support of the classical-Christian tradition for its preservation. The possibility of civility, then, depends upon the flourishing of institutions that preserve the tradition that is the source of civility. I argue that civility requires nonpoliticized, nonideological, free social institutions, including and especially universities and churches.

Although my focus is on Montaigne, I intend to shed light on the fundamental orientation of modern philosophy as such. In spite of the differences among modern philosophers, it is possible to identify a unity of purpose: the mastery of nature and the emancipation of man by man. Modernity, as Rémi Brague argues, is a "project." In *The Kingdom of Man: Genesis and Failure of the Modern Project*, he notes that the beginning of the period that we call "modern" is marked by "an increased prevalence of words that designate 'essay,' 'attempt,' 'experience' in the sense of 'experiment.'"[5] This is most evident in Montaigne's *Essays*, the experiment that is the modern project.

Brague writes: "A project implies (1) vis-à-vis the past, the idea of a new beginning which causes the forgetting of everything that preceded; (2) vis-à-vis the present, the idea of the autonomy of the acting subject; and (3) for the future, the idea of a supportive milieu that prolongs the action and ensures its successful completion (progress)."[6] The chapters of my book reflect Brague's outline of the modern project: Montaigne's "science of forgetfulness" of the tradition and his new beginning of philosophy in the act of "reflection"; authenticity as the mode of being of the autonomous subject; and civility as the supportive milieu for the progress of freedom and equality. In chapters 1 through 4, I set out Montaigne's invention of civility, how civility originates, and what civility is. In chapters 5 and 6, I discuss the inevitable deterioration of civility and the disintegration of the social bond.

In the first chapter, I introduce the "new Adam," created by the new type of philosopher, through the sleight-of-hand of philosophical reflection and invention. I show how philosophy appears in the *Essays* against the background of the premodern tradition with its understanding of philosophy as theoretical contemplation. The tradition that Montaigne attacks is the classical-Christian tradition, which is essentially Aristotelian at the time of the Reformation. Montaigne refers to Aristotle as "the god of scholastic philosophy" (VS539, F403),[7] whose authority has been placed beyond question. The cracks that Montaigne sees in the foundation of the tradition, cracks that eventually led to its collapse, are the weaknesses of the first principles of Aristotle's philosophy. In general, the philosophers of the early modern period have these Aristotelian first principles as their target. When I refer to "the tradition," I mean this tradition articulated by Aristotle, and I take Josef Pieper's writings on tradition and culture as accurately describing and explaining that tradition.

The world Montaigne inherited was a world of violent civil and religious conflict in which the social bond of the sacred tradition seemed too weak to prevent the complete dissolution of the civilization of Christendom. When Montaigne retires to his study to write his essays, he uncovers the foundation of this civilization in order to see its weakness and to replace it with a new civilization built on a solid philosophical foundation.

I argue that the foundation of the tradition, as Montaigne sees it, is the direction of human being to the divine. Divine worship is the origin of leisure, which frees the human being for the pursuit of the "higher things"—that is, for philosophy and politics. The fundamental distinction between activities that are "free" and activities that are "servile" is the basis for the hierarchy of leisure and work that structured the premodern world. The "common good" requires that some must be slaves—that is, devoted to servile occupations—so that gentlemen and philosophers might be free to pursue the higher things. The fault that Montaigne uncovers in the foundation of classical-Christian civilization is this justification of the master-slave condition.

Montaigne wants to replace that foundation with a philosophical foundation for equality and freedom. Therefore, his first and most fundamental task is the transformation of philosophy itself. The modern philosophical act, as it appears in the *Essays*, erases the distinction between free and servile activities, thus undermining the justification for the hierarchy of leisure and work.

The first step in Montaigne's freeing himself from the tradition is the reduction of sacred tradition to mere human custom, denying the divine origin of tradition and showing it to be merely arbitrary and contingent. Tradition is the prejudice that must be put aside if we are to see the world as it really is. Once the authority of tradition over the human mind has been called into question, philosophy can become "self-conscious."

The modern philosophical act, as Montaigne displays it, is twofold. Montaigne describes himself as "detached" from himself and "spying" on himself. This act is at the heart of modern philosophy. It is the act in which the philosopher becomes the detached observer, removing himself from participation in the tradition. In this moment of radical skepticism, everything suddenly appears as unknown, and the natural mind becomes visible to the philosopher. This is the act of philosophical "reflection" (the mind observing itself), the moment of philosophical self-consciousness.

When the philosopher is separated from the natural man, the natural man no longer appears as a human form ordered to a naturally given end. Rather the natural man is now seen to be merely a collection of "accidents" in no given order. The second moment of the philosophical act, then, is the act of judgment that reorders these accidents to an end determined by the human will. This reordering is the mastery of nature, and of human nature in particular, which is the essence of the modern project. The new Adam, then, is not the created being who stands in wondering contemplation of the world and its Creator, but the judge who orders all things in accordance with his will.

In the second chapter, I set out what this transition from contemplation to judgment means. Montaigne redirects the human being away from the divine to man himself and thus effects the most radical change in the meaning of the good. The good "in itself" and "for its own sake" becomes "value," the good in relation to man as man. All things are now revalued according to the standard of man as man, not according to the standard of the tradition, nature, and the divine.

The good that Montaigne seeks to produce is the resolution of the conflict between weak and strong, masters and slaves, which can only be accomplished through the reformation of *mores*. The strong must give up their natural claim to mastery in the act of voluntary submission that Michael Oakeshott calls "the moralization of pride."[8] The "great," the noble gentlemen, must renounce pride and the desire for recognition and honor, so that all submit to the new moral and political order on equal terms. Montaigne himself is the first to do this, and he displays this possibility in the *Essays*.

I argue that the modern political order brought into being by this act of submission is the new liberal order. The term "liberalism" has taken very different meanings over its history. I stipulate that what I mean by "liberalism" is the modern form of political life embodied in the distinction and relation between state and society. The state is the new invisible master to which all must submit, the authority brought into being in the modern philosophical act through which man now rules himself. In concrete terms, the state takes the form of representative government and the rule of law, and society is the sphere in which the individual is left free to pursue the good as he sees fit.

While the standard of the common good was the measure of just and unjust regimes in the premodern world, Montaigne rejects the idea of the common good as the pretext for the domination of the strong over the weak. He argues that, since philosophy has not been able to find a way to the common good, "let each one seek it in his particularity" (VS622, F471). Society is the arena in which the individual is free to seek the satisfaction of his particularity. I argue that liberalism so understood is put forward in the *Essays* as the new form of human association in which civility is the social bond.

In chapters 3 and 4, I set out the moral character that is necessary and suited for this new liberal order: authenticity and civility. Although Montaigne never uses the term "authenticity," when he asserts that "the greatest thing in the world is to know how to belong to oneself" (VS242, F178), he is giving expression to what will come to be known as authenticity more than three centuries later. Authenticity is the condition for civility: civility is the way in which the individual who knows how to belong to himself is related to others in civil society.

Authenticity is the form of moral life that replaces traditional moral virtue, the moral virtue that had been understood as the perfection and completion of human nature in its attainment of its naturally given end. The human being who must seek the good in his particularity can no longer understand himself as a member of the species sharing a common human nature. Individuals are "incommensurable" particulars, each conferring value on what he chooses and making himself to be what he wants to be. The individual is then complete in himself.

In Montaigne's terms, the authentic individual is the "self-ordered" soul. That is, he is not directed by nature to an end that he does not choose but orders himself to himself. The authentic individual does not need other men for the good life: he is satisfied within himself, living a private life. "Greatness" has been transformed from the public display of noble deeds to the hiddenness of self-possession.

But the price of this unprecedented freedom of the individual to make himself what he wants to be is the disappearance of any public moral standard and the impossibility of moral community. How are such individuals, who do not need each other for the good life, to live together in peace?

Civility replaces the social bond of the tradition in the absence of the possibility of moral community. In chapter 4, I set out the way in which civility forms the new social bond from the fragments of the classical-Christian tradition, especially classical magnanimity and Christian charity. These fragments are now reordered to the good of man as man—that is, to settling the conflict between masters and slaves by purely human means. Civility is the suppression of the natural human self through the overcoming of the natural desire for mastery and the acceptance of un-natural equality. The noblemen, the gentlemen, must be eliminated, and the slaves liberated. Montaigne's "elimination of the gentlemen" is accomplished through his reformation of mores.[9]

A *civil* society is a society from which the political struggle for rule has been eliminated. So the suppression of the natural desire for mastery is the first condition for civility. Public life is the arena in which men struggle for honor and recognition through the display of superiority in the practice of the moral virtues such as courage and justice. Montaigne says that he freely chooses a private life and stays out of politics on account of his conscience. He does not seek his good in public life, and his service to his prince is "limited and conditional" according to the demands of his conscience (VS794, F603).

The suppression of the natural desire for mastery appears in the *Essays* as the separation of the man from the prince, the interiorization of honor, the deliberate preference for private life, and the privatization of conscience. Taken together, these radical departures from the tradition amount to the privatization of morality. And the privatization of morality means that there is no public standard of morality, there are no public standards of honor and shame, and therefore there is no possibility of moral community.

Civil society is an association of equals, each having the right to seek the good in his particularity. Therefore, each individual must acknowledge the others as equal to him even though they are not equal by nature.

Civility, in this condition of equality, might be described as "loyalty" to one another that takes the form of a disposition to live under the laws as equals, even though the laws, which are not made with reference to any universal moral standard and are not concerned with justice in the traditional sense, are not perfectly just. Civility itself, then, cannot be legislated, for it is the more fundamental determination to accept equality under the law.

Montaigne's will to accept this unnatural equality is grounded in the way he judges himself and others. In fact, he claims that his way of judging is new and unique. He judges each man as he is in himself, in his particularity. Further, his judgment is generous, for he assumes the presence of a good will in everyone. The elements of civility flow from his generosity of judgment. In particular, civility entails the trust that is necessary in the everyday interactions of free individuals. The elements of civility are the determination to keep one's promises, the mutual forgiveness of insults, toleration, openness of heart, and the generosity of self-revelation. Civility elevates social interaction above the merely servile and useful, making these interactions morally satisfying in themselves. The moral virtues of the tradition, necessary for life in a political community, are replaced by the "social virtues" desirable for life in modern society.

In the new liberal order, philosophy becomes "sociable wisdom" (VS1116, F857), an act of the self-revelation that forms the social bond. For Montaigne, philosophy begins in the desire to reveal himself and ends in the self-revelation of his new particularity, the moral character that makes society possible. Sociable wisdom helps to make society civil, elevating it above the political struggle and covering over the naked force of the power of the state.

In chapters 5 and 6, I discuss the deterioration of civility and the disintegration of the social bond. The failure of civility is a moral disaster that causes us to try to understand how and why it happened. The ways in which civility has failed reveal to us more clearly just what the sources of civility are and just what is necessary for civility to endure. I argue that civility fails because it originates in the forgetfulness of the classical-Christian tradition from which the elements of civility are taken. Cut off from their source, cut off from the whole in which they have their meaning, these elements wither and die.

In chapter 5, I discuss the free institutions and practices that are necessary to support the civil disposition. Montaigne himself saw the importance of these free institutions and practices. Civility is the social bond of a free society: only a free society can be a civil society. The sociologist who has studied civility most thoroughly, Edward Shils, insists on the role of the social institutions of family, church, and university for the preservation of civil society. These institutions are "the internal spine"[10] of the culture that maintains a society, and they must be left as free as possible from the coercive power of the state if civility is to be fostered and kept alive.

The greatest internal threat to free institutions is the politicization of society that occurs when tradition is replaced by ideology. An ideology, in contrast to tradition, is an abstract principle or system of ideas that sets out a goal of perfection, an "ideal," which can never be achieved in practice but nevertheless orients the entire society to its realization. Ideology enters into and rules every aspect of social life, destroying the freedom of social institutions and the free expression of thought. I discuss the current suppression of free speech and the suffocating force of "political correctness," which is always defended as necessary for civility but is actually inimical to civility.

The threat to free speech is most evident in the universities and colleges where the goal of the pursuit of truth has been replaced by the ideology of social justice. If liberal education is to foster civility, it must remain above the political conflicts of the day. I argue against the claim that the purpose of liberal education is to foster "critical thinking." While "critical thinking" can admit of many interpretations, it is most often taken to mean criticizing the tradition, rejecting the study of the great books, unmasking them as the sources of oppression, racism, sexism, and so on. The education that Montaigne recommends is the formation of judgment, not the purely destructive practice of "critical thinking." The formation of judgment actually requires the appropriation of the tradition in the formation of one's character. The deterioration of civility reveals what is essential to civility: the free exchange of ideas and the preservation of the tradition in education.

The disintegration of the social bond occurs when the conditions for the preservation of the classical and Christian sources of civility are suppressed and ultimately disappear. The disintegration of civility, then, is due to the suppression of honor, which keeps nobility alive, and the suppression of religion, which keeps Christian charity alive. In chapters 1 through 4, I emphasize the suppression of honor in the hiddenness of authenticity, in the privatization of morality, and in the civil disposition itself.

In chapter 6, I discuss the disintegration of the social bond in terms of the disappearance of religion from public life. Many philosophers and sociologists who have studied civility (whether or not they themselves are believers) acknowledge that sacred tradition is the source of the respect for and recognition of the dignity of the individual that are essential for civility.

The social bond of medieval Europe was the divine liturgy, in which all members of the society participated and where social distinctions counted for nothing in the presence of the Eucharist. The Reformation shattered the unity of Christendom and initiated the privatization of faith. Modern political philosophers recognized the importance of religion for the social bond but subordinated religion to the state. With the Enlightenment, religion became purely instrumental, and the explicit connection to the divine was broken. Voltaire, for example, held that there could be a new universal morality without dependence on divine revelation. Rousseau's "civil religion" is religion reduced to principles of sociability. Kant's religion within the limits of reason alone is the elimination of traditional Christianity. Finally, postmodernism demands a purely secular society from which all traces of religion are removed.

Montaigne himself does see the importance of religion for the social bond. He criticizes the Reformation for its privatization of religion, and he looks to the Church as a universal society, "the great common way" (VS520, F387). In this context, I discuss the problem of the assimilation of Muslims in Europe and America. The abandonment of Christianity in the West, the secularization of Western society, and the failure of the universities to preserve the tradition mean that we have little to offer to Muslims who might be open to the alternative of a tradition grounded in the harmony of faith and reason.

I conclude this discussion of the failure of civility by returning to the origins of the modern project and Montaigne's project in particular. As Pascal insists, civility is not the annihilation but merely the suppression and concealment of the human self as the natural desire for mastery of the strong over the weak.[11] When this human self reemerges, without the constraints of the tradition, the fragile bond of civility becomes impossible to maintain. The disintegration of the social bond manifests itself most clearly in the reemergence of the master-slave relationship in contemporary life. I rely here on Rémi Brague's description of the failure of the modern project: the intention of man to be master of himself eventuates in the domination of a certain type of human being over other, "lesser" human beings. I also rely on Patrick Deneen's account of the new aristocracy of the domination of the strong over the weak that comes into existence chiefly out of our contemporary educational system.[12] My claim is that the authentic "self-creators" become a new elite, and the distance between this new aristocracy and those who cling to the tradition becomes so great that there can be no bond between them. The reemergence of the master-slave dynamic, in all its naked brutality and cruelty, and without the possibility of appeal to the restraints of the tradition, shows that, more than anything else, it is the suppression of religion that destroys civility.

The claim that the public presence of religion is essential for the preservation of civility, however, assumes that the churches themselves have not fallen under the influence of political ideology and that they have maintained their direction to the divine. As Daniel Mahoney has argued, Christianity is subverted by the religion of humanity.[13] If Christianity is reduced to a kind of humanism, if Christian charity is reduced to a free-floating compassion, the ultimate result is unspeakable cruelty. To paraphrase Flannery O'Connor, when compassion is detached from the true source of compassion, the outcome is terror, the concentration camp, and the gas chambers.[14]

The disintegration of the social bond of civility is the collapse of the world Montaigne made. Although he offered supports for civility in his presentation of the civil character, in his vision of liberal education, and in his recognition of the need for the public presence of religion, civility was bound to fail, because its invention undermined the public power of the tradition, the very source of the moral content of civility.

Where, then, can we look for help in understanding our own condition? Recent attempts to recover the tradition through the return to Aristotle and Aquinas have brought out the meaning of moral virtue, the common good, and natural law in their relevance for the recovery of moral community. These attempts help us to see what has been lost and, in some cases, how we might recover what has been lost.

I suggest that in this our postmodern, post-Christian world, we can also look to Pascal, who saw clearly the dangers of the modern project with respect to human beings. Like all early modern philosophers, Pascal broke with the Scholastic-Aristotelian view of nature. But in spite of this rejection of Aristotle, and against the Protestant Reformation, he insists that "tradition is the true source of truth."[15] Pascal offers us a way into the tradition that is more Augustinian than Thomistic. He sees civility as merely the suppression of the human self, not the true annihilation of the self that can only occur through Christian piety. And he sees with exceptional clarity the nature of human power and the limits of politics.

ONE

The New Adam

The Philosopher's Sleight of Hand

THE WORLD MONTAIGNE INHERITED: MASTERS AND SLAVES

The world from which Montaigne retired in 1580 to write his "essays" was a world of violent civil and religious conflict. As he tells us, "The innovations of Luther were beginning to gain favor and to shake our old beliefs in many places" (VS439, F320). At the same time, it was a world in which the learned were rediscovering the riches of ancient philosophy, breaking free of the authority of Aristotle, and the "humanists" were freeing philosophy from its servitude to theology. It must have seemed that the very foundation of civilization was shaken and crumbling, exposing the weakness that must have been there from the beginning, a weakness that had finally revealed itself in the destruction of the social bond.

What is this social bond, and what is the foundation that formed the world Montaigne inherited? The foundation of classical-Christian civilization is the sacred tradition, the intellectual and moral inheritance that embodies a certain understanding of Being, of nature, and of man's place in nature. Sacred tradition is not simply custom: there can be many customs and many "traditions" of the arts, of individual families, and of voluntary associations, and many "traditions" of philosophical thought to which individuals and groups might adhere. Sacred tradition, as I discuss it here, is not just one among many "traditions," for sacred tradition is the social bond that is public, common, and authoritative for all. It is not simply a customary way of doing things that is useful for the practices of everyday life. Rather, sacred tradition "concerns the center of the world and the core of [our] own existence."[1] It has this great power and authority because it is not a human invention or creation but begins by a divine transmission, and the truth that it carries is uncreated truth.[2] Tradition, as Pascal says, is "the true source of truth."[3]

Eamon Duffy, in *The Stripping of the Altars*, shows in historical detail how the traditional religion of pre-Reformation Europe actually did form a very strong social bond. The sacraments of the Church brought about the interweaving of the sacred and the social that is the lived reality of sacred tradition. Duffy insists on "the social homogeneity of late medieval religion."[4] As he demonstrates, "Rich and poor, simple and sophisticate could kneel side by side, using the same prayers and sharing the same hopes." In spite of the differences of sophistication about the faith, "they did not have a different religion."[5] The social bond of medieval Europe was found in the divine liturgy, in the celebration of the Eucharist, where the loftiest theologian was at one with the least educated laborer, for the tradition was what was common to all.

Josef Pieper claims: "Real unity among human beings has its roots in nothing else but the common possession of [sacred] tradition."[6] If tradition were merely a human invention, it could have no authority and no power to unite, to bind men to each other, beyond any other human convention. To bind men, it must be acknowledged to be higher than any human convention or agreement. Tradition implies community, the union not only of those now living but of those who have lived in the past and those who will live in the future. It binds the generations of men to each other in the transmission of truth. Therefore, tradition must be a publicly shared way of life. "Tradition, then, means the memory of the community which gives the people of God their self-understanding."[7]

The sacred tradition that forms the social bond of Western civilization through the Middle Ages, as Montaigne confronted it, is Aristotelian and Thomistic. The *Essays* reveal that this is Montaigne's understanding. Although he refers to many philosophers and schools of philosophy, his principal target in his rejection of the tradition is Aristotle and the Thomistic appropriation of Aristotle because of the hold that Aristotle had over the minds of his day. The philosophy of Aristotle, as appropriated by scholastic theologians such as Thomas Aquinas, was the teaching that dominated the universities.[8] Montaigne complains that "the god of scholastic knowledge is Aristotle; . . . his authority is the end beyond which it is not permitted to inquire" (VS539, F403). Therefore, accepted philosophical beliefs are never questioned but are discussed only to be supported and confirmed. This presumption is both the constraint on the liberty of our judgments and the tyranny over our beliefs. Aristotle's first principles have become our presuppositions, and "whoever is believed in his presuppositions, he is our master and our God; he will plant his foundations so broad and easy that by them he will be able to raise us, if he wants, up to the clouds" (VS539–40, F403–4).

The major outlines of the tradition that Montaigne inherits and rejects must be set out in terms of Aristotle's first principles. The structure of classical-Christian civilization is the hierarchy of leisure and work. In *Leisure the Basis of Culture*, Josef Pieper presents a Platonic-Aristotelian-Thomistic account of leisure as the foundation of Western civilization, an account that accords with Montaigne's perception of the tradition. Leisure has its origin in divine worship that is both public and common. It is a setting aside of time from the necessities of work and labor, from servile occupations, and devoting that time to the divine and the eternal. That is why the observance of the Sabbath requires that we abstain from all work. Leisure must be distinguished not only from work but also from both idleness and play: from idleness because leisure is a kind of activity and from play because leisure is an attitude of mind, a habit of turning the mind toward "the higher things."

Sacred tradition is a way of life that embodies a certain understanding of the human good. The actions that fulfill the human being, that actualize his being most fully, cannot be the actions that merely serve his life, for such actions are not distinctively human but belong to all animals. This distinction between activities that serve the needs of life and those that are distinctively human is the basis for the hierarchy of leisure and work. This hierarchy of the activities of leisure and work can be seen even in the physical layout of the city as it is presented in Aristotle's description of the best city. At the highest point are situated the temples, "buildings assigned for divine matters." Immediately below the temples is the "market," but this is the market that is "free" of wares, the market for "being at leisure" where the free men gather to discuss and argue at leisure and to observe each other and become acquainted with each other's characters. Below this is the market in the ordinary sense of buying and selling.[9]

We can distinguish between the actions proper to leisure and the actions proper to work in terms of the difference between activities that are ends in themselves and those that have their end outside the activity, the distinction made in the very first words of Aristotle's *Ethics* and the fundamental distinction underlying his account of the good life: "The good is that at which all things aim. But there appears to be a certain difference among the ends: some ends are activities, others are certain works apart from the activities themselves."[10] The naturally given end of all human activity is the good, and the activities that are proper to man are "good in themselves" or ends in themselves. To be "within" the tradition is to live within this distinction between actions and within this orientation to the good.

What does it mean to say that an action is an end in itself? Activities that are ends in themselves are said to be "for their own sake," not for the sake of some result that will follow from them. Actions that are ends in themselves are "complete in themselves" and do not produce anything outside themselves.[11] Rather, they change the condition of the agent himself, perfect the agent in himself, bring him to fulfillment, and therefore satisfy him, not because he has chosen them but because of what he is, his nature as a human being. In other words, the worth of these activities does not depend upon human choice but on their intrinsic worth within the natural order.

Actions that are ends in themselves are of two kinds: theoretical (the activity of philosophy) and moral (the practice of the moral virtues). The theoretical is higher than the moral, because it is the fulfillment of what is highest in man, his intellect. For Aristotle, philosophy is indeed the participation in the divine activity of "thought thinking thought," so that the philosopher is the man who, by his nature, shares in the divine. The moral, on the other hand, is entirely human, for it involves the rule of reason over the passions and the rule of men over each other.

Both the life of contemplation and the life of moral virtue require freedom from work, from subjection to the necessities of life. Freedom, in the classical world, is not freedom *from* nature but a freedom that remains within nature, the freedom of engagement in activities that are ends in themselves that are given by nature.

That leisure is the condition for philosophy is set forth at the beginning of Aristotle's *Metaphysics*. The sciences, and philosophy in particular, were discovered where men first began to have leisure. The theoretical stance toward the world is possible when men are freed from the necessities of production to pursue knowledge "for its own sake." When the philosopher takes the "theoretical attitude" toward the world, he steps beyond the realm of necessity and work in order to see the world as it is in itself, not in relation to his needs and wants. "It was when almost all the necessities of life and the things that make for comfort and recreation had been secured, that such knowledge began to be sought. Evidently then we do not seek it for the sake of any other advantage; but as the man is free, we say, who exists for his own sake and not for another's, so we pursue this as the only free science, for it alone exists for its own sake."[12] Philosophy is free because it is useless; that is, it serves no end outside itself. The freedom of the philosopher, then, is the freedom of engaging in action that is an end in itself.

Philosophy begins in wonder, and this beginning shows that the knowledge it seeks is knowledge for its own sake. The philosopher does not want to change the world but simply to understand it in its first causes. For the philosopher, the satisfaction of wonder is found in contemplation, the natural fulfillment of the mind *because* it is knowledge for its own sake. The natural wonder at why things are the way they are is satisfied in contemplation of the first causes of all things. Leisure is the *receptive* attitude of the mind toward being, and contemplation is the act in which the world is brought into the mind: the mind becomes what it knows.

Aristotle's account of philosophy as theoretical contemplation is an account given by a philosopher who remains within the tradition as a participant. To engage in this theoretical activity of philosophy is to participate in the tradition, because the tradition is this understanding of human completion.

For classical-Christian philosophy, it is tradition that makes philosophy possible. Josef Pieper explains that philosophy means thinking about "the whole of what meets us in experience from every possible aspect in its fundamental significance." The individual who practices philosophy "*keeps a question open* and thinks it through methodically." This person "stands *as a person* in a tradition and participates in it as a believing hearer. . . . Insofar as I as a person am actually participating in a tradition, or to put it another way, insofar as I actually accept [what is handed down in] sacred tradition as truth . . . , then and only then do I have the capacity to practice philosophy seriously"—that is, to consider my subject under any possible aspect.[13] Tradition "keeps open" the questions that every man asks because these questions arise within the tradition. To stand in and to participate in a tradition is not to *judge* the tradition but to accept what is given in sacred tradition, to trust in the givenness of truth.

Pieper discusses the concept of tradition in terms of the distinction between sacred tradition and tradition in the broader sense of what is in any way handed down—that is, the distinction between "The Tradition" and "traditions." He argues that "there is in the last analysis only *one* traditional good that it is absolutely necessary to preserve unchanged, namely the gift that is received and handed on in the *sacred* tradition."[14]

However, the character of sacred tradition is such that it becomes intertwined with all aspects of life, so that what is truly essential to it can be difficult to discern. On the one hand, it requires great caution to undertake the smallest changes even in customs that do not appear to be directly related to the essence. On the other hand, it is this distinction between the essence of sacred tradition and its nonessential accretions that sometimes makes possible even significant changes in custom. Pieper explains that "a 'cultivation of tradition' that attaches itself to a historically accidental external image of what has been handed down becomes a positive hindrance to a real transmission of what is truly worth conserving, which perhaps can occur only under changed historical forms. It is possible to imagine a real transmission of what is in the last analysis worth handing down, which a dogmatic conservatism could not even recognize."[15] Both ancient and medieval culture understood the human being as oriented to the divine: Aristotle, for example, held that philosophy, the highest human activity, is in some sense divine. Thus, Plato, Aristotle, Augustine, and Aquinas differ greatly in their philosophical claims and judgments about the world, but all adhere to the same tradition, the tradition that sees man as oriented to the divine.

Therefore, although it might seem that acceptance of tradition places constraints on the freedom of philosophical inquiry, tradition does not limit or restrict philosophical questioning. Rather, it preserves wonder and mystery, for it hands down a truth that is not limited by the human mind. Tradition is the recognition of the mysterious character of the world.[16] Philosophy is about understanding the tradition more deeply *because* tradition is the divinely given source of truth. Tradition preserves the core of truth for the human mind. That core of truth has to do with the relationship of the human being to the divine.

Leisure is also the condition for moral perfection, which is found in the practice of virtue "for its own sake." Moral virtue is attained in the development of a noble rather than a servile character. The practice of servile actions associated with work, labor, buying, and selling has an effect on the soul, making it incapable of noble action: servile actions turn the mind toward the useful, not the honorable or noble. Noble actions rise above the useful and are "for their own sake," not for the sake of their results or for the sake of glory. Yet they do bring glory and honor because they benefit the city as a whole. The moral virtues of courage and justice, for example, perfect the soul of the individual and, at the same time, serve the entire political community. The city exists not merely for the pleasure that might come from living with others, but for the sake of noble actions through which men distinguish themselves and display their individuality and superiority.[17] The city is the space for the struggle for recognition, especially the struggle over who deserves to rule. That is why honor plays such an important role in political life.

The city is "complete" in that it contains within itself everything necessary for the good of the human being, both his biological and his distinctively human needs. It is only in the political association that human beings can find their perfection and completion, for the city exists not merely for the sake of life itself, but for the good life.[18] Aristotle insists that the natural end of the city is the "common good." The standard of the common good implies a very strong notion of community. The common good is a hierarchical relationship of mutual dependence. Men depend upon each other not only for the necessities of life but for moral virtue as well. Moral community requires a visible hierarchy of moral excellence grounded in the standard of "the good in itself."

The classical philosopher sees himself within the cosmos and within the city. Within the cosmos, the philosopher is united with all men because his activity is the completion and perfection of what all men possess. Aristotle begins his metaphysics with the assertion that "all men by nature desire to know." The philosopher is an animal, like all other men. There is a continuity between the human senses and the knowledge that the philosopher seeks. The philosopher participates in the divine activity of contemplation as a human, natural being, as a member of the animal species.

Within the city, philosophy depends upon leisure, and leisure has its origin in divine worship. Insofar as all are united in divine worship, philosophy is not separated from human community. Aristotle refers to the city as the *political community*.[19] What makes it *political* is the arrangement and the nature of the relationship of rulers and ruled. What makes the city a *community* is the presence and practice of the activities of leisure. A community is an association in which the members depend upon each other for the good life and in which the good life is more than the relationship of ruling and being ruled. The philosopher needs other men; he depends upon workers, including slaves, for the needs of life. But the other members of the community also need the philosopher, for he instantiates and preserves the "higher things" for the sake of which the city exists. The coherence of the political community depends upon the recognition of what is higher and better than the political struggle over rule; that is, it depends upon religion and philosophy. Therefore, as Pieper insists, philosophical contemplation is an essential component of the common good: "It is necessary for the perfection of human society that there should be men who devote their lives to contemplation."[20] The city cannot be complete and the good cannot be common without the public presence of leisure and the higher things.

With Christianity, philosophy becomes the "handmaiden" of theology, and contemplation becomes union with the divine in prayer and worship. Classical moral virtue is understood to be perfected in the theological virtues of faith, hope, and charity. Nevertheless, the standard of the common good, the place of contemplation in human community, and the hierarchy of leisure and work persisted through the Middle Ages into the early modern world.

When Montaigne looks at the world he inherited, he sees a very different scene from the one presented by Pieper. He sees the tradition as the mask covering over a much different reality, the mastery of the weak by the strong. For Montaigne, the idea of the common good is simply the "pretext of reason" for the actions of vicious men (VS802, F609–10). In reality, the weak are simply at the mercy of the strong. Contrary to Aristotle, rule is always the domination of masters over slaves.

The fault and weakness that Montaigne sees in the foundation of classical-Christian civilization comes to light when we consider the place of philosophy in the city. Philosophy is a participant in the common good, but it is not a participant in the political struggle over who should rule. Indeed, it is an essential constituent of the common good *because* it is not a participant in the political struggle, because it is not a partisan and does not put forth a claim in the struggle over who should rule. It is present as something that stands above politics, and therefore as something that makes the good "common." Francis Slade says of premodern political philosophy: "Most of all it is concerned to point out that there is something better than ruling over human beings; that the best kind of activity is not ruling but contemplative knowing, and thus to show that rule has an intrinsic limit; and consequently that the attempt to derive fulfillment from it commensurate with what is the highest in man is endless and futile."[21]

Pieper argues that leisure and philosophy are essential to human dignity and freedom, for they manifest the fact that the human being is not simply an instrument to be used by others. The establishment of the non-instrumental nature of the human is, in principle, then, a safeguard against tyranny: tyranny is the master-slave relationship writ large. The freedom of philosophy, the freedom of the theoretical, from the necessities of life, is a freedom that affects the entire community because it stands as the principle that men cannot be reduced to means, that the human being is more than servile and useful, serving an end outside himself. Further, leisure has its origin in religion, specifically in divine worship that removes not only the philosopher but all of the citizens from the world of work. If the completion and perfection of human nature is freedom from the merely useful, then human nature as such possesses that inherent dignity of being above and greater than the merely useful.[22]

However, it might be argued that the practice of slavery in Greek civilization—and the hierarchy of leisure and work itself—stand as the great contradiction to Pieper's account and prove that philosophy is ineffective in protecting human freedom and dignity. The leisure that allows the emergence of philosophy is possible only on the condition that some are slaves and exist for the sake of the masters. In book 1 of the *Politics* Aristotle does provide a defense of the practice of slavery. However, it is a very restrained and limited defense. Slavery is just only when it is natural, and it is natural only when the slave is not capable of existing for himself and when the natural inequality between master and slave is so great that the slave also benefits from the relationship. Aristotle goes so far as to say that, in those cases, there can even be a kind of friendship between masters and slaves. But, in fact, slaves in Greek cities were captives taken by force in war and were not necessarily slaves "by nature."

Aristotle, then, judges as unjust precisely that practice, slavery, which makes possible the leisure that is the condition for philosophy. He does not justify conventional slavery, but he accepts this condition. The philosopher's teaching about the natural order of justice is ineffective. Nor is it intended to be effective, for philosophy's contribution to the common good is to be above rule. Premodern political philosophy, then, practices moderation and restraint in what it expects of politics and what it expects of itself with respect to politics. It does not seek to rule. But for modern philosophy, this restraint appears as weakness and powerlessness.[23]

Modern philosophy is ashamed of the weakness of premodern philosophy. From the perspective of modern philosophy, philosophy as contemplation is weak and shameful because it does not effect the common good. It is supposed to be a limit on rule, but it is without any real power, for the common good is never and can never really be achieved. Rather, the appeal to "the common good" is the deception used by the strong to dominate the weak.

Montaigne exhibits the shame of modern philosophy for the weakness of contemplation in his essay entitled "Of Idleness." Here he is playing on the traditional notions of leisure and contemplation, conflating leisure with idleness. By identifying leisure with mere idleness, Montaigne calls into question the very basis of classical culture. Idleness, in the tradition, is the opposite of leisure. Whereas leisure is devoted to the highest things, Montaigne makes leisure appear frivolous and vain: leisure is merely "play." He tells us that when he retired to solitude from public life, he wanted to let his mind entertain itself in leisure. Leisure, then, is not the mind's attitude when contemplating the divine, but the mind alone with itself amusing itself. Montaigne is ashamed of the fact that leisure "does" nothing. In writing his essays, he is "hoping in time to make [his] mind ashamed of itself" (VS33, F21).

When Montaigne retires to his study to write his essays, he makes a new world. He overcomes the foundational distinction between actions that are ends in themselves and actions that produce effects by transforming the philosophical act itself into the act of philosophical invention that brings the new world into being.

The New Figure of the Philosopher

The new, modern philosopher wants to change the world, to master nature, not simply to know it. In order to change the world, to master nature, the philosopher must be able to extricate himself from nature, to rise above nature, in a sense, so as to have power over nature. Philosophy must become free in a radically new way. It can no longer be satisfied with a freedom that remains within nature and tradition. The freedom of philosophy cannot be *given* to it by nature or by tradition. The philosopher must seize this freedom and this power for himself by his own act.

The new freedom of philosophy is captured in the experience of philosophical "self-consciousness." When philosophy becomes self-conscious, man is complete in himself, having freed himself from tradition, from nature, and from divine revelation. What does this self-consciousness entail? How does this experience differ from the experience of premodern philosophy?

Premodern philosophy is not "self-conscious." In "The Origin of Philosophical Self-Consciousness," Gerhard Kruger argues that the premodern philosopher is absorbed in the contemplation of being, of God and of nature. He is not conscious of himself, but loses himself in the object of contemplation. The mind of the philosopher is receptive to what is given to it in nature and in the tradition. The modern philosopher, on the contrary, turns back to himself, to his own mind, in a reflexive action.[24] This reflexive action is entirely his own act. By nature, the mind of the philosopher is drawn out by wonder to know the whole of all that is. The mind is not immediately concerned to know itself. The turn back to his own mind is not natural but rather an act of freeing itself from nature.

The fundamental difference between premodern and modern philosophical freedom is that, for modern philosophy, "philosophical freedom is *self-conscious*."[25] As Francis Slade explains, the ancient philosopher engaged in philosophy, but he did not know himself as the origin of philosophy, because he is not the origin, for it is given by nature. The modern philosopher, on the other hand, knows himself as the origin of philosophy: he knows philosophy as "his own actual deed." Modern philosophy "is the creation of the philosopher, something established by his own act. . . . Philosophy is not something given with the givenness of man, but a manifestation of human freedom." This means that philosophy creates its own possibility, that it generates itself and is self-constituted.[26] Man, then, is complete in himself and takes possession of himself, freeing himself from nature and tradition and taking possession of his own mind in self-consciousness.

The self-consciousness described by Kruger and by Slade is the defining characteristic of modern philosophy as such. Philosophy's new freedom from nature is the condition for the mastery of nature that is the goal of modern epistemology and modern natural science. Montaigne's focus, however, is not the nonhuman natural world of the scientist but the human world of morals and politics. His project is nothing less than the mastery and transformation of human nature itself.

How does modern philosophical self-consciousness manifest itself in Montaigne's *Essays*? Montaigne describes himself as a philosopher only once. When the desire to reveal himself seizes him, he calls on the help of ancient philosophy to show himself in public. His thoughts, his "caprices," are new, born with him, and "without a model." But when he expresses them spontaneously, in public, they seem to resemble the "humors" of ancient philosophy. His mores or ways of being are weak, but when he reveals them, he is surprised to see that they resemble, by accident, the teachings and examples of traditional philosophy. To his astonishment, he finds that he is "a new figure: an unpremeditated and accidental philosopher!" (VS546, F409). The philosophical act brings into being a new figure of the philosopher out of the fragments of the shattered tradition. He becomes conscious of himself as a new kind of philosopher.

Unpremeditated and accidental philosophy both reveals and conceals him. His accidental similarity to ancient philosophy and to the teachings of Christianity makes him visible. Montaigne uses the tradition of ancient philosophy and Christianity, masters it, subjects it, in order to reveal his particularity as a man, the man who happens to be the philosopher. He expresses what he is in the fragments of the classical-Christian philosophical tradition. At the same time, the fragments of the tradition hide him, because they cover over what is his own, his "originality." So he just looks like a patchwork of these pieces of skepticism, Stoicism, Epicureanism, Plato, Aristotle, Plutarch, Augustine, and many others.

Unpremeditated and accidental philosophy does not begin in wonder but in the desire to reveal himself. It ends not in wondering contemplation of Being, but in astonishment at himself. In this account of his astonishing discovery of himself as a new kind of philosopher, he reveals the meaning of modern philosophical self-consciousness.

What is Montaigne doing in the interval between the desire that seizes him to reveal himself and the actual revelation of himself as the new figure of the philosopher? This hidden interval is where his originality lies and the modern philosophical act occurs.

The first step in Montaigne's achievement of self-consciousness is the liberation of himself from the power of tradition. Kruger says that "the modern freedom of philosophy . . . is primarily set against what is *pronounced with authority*"—that is, tradition. The tradition that forms and is authoritative for the premodern understanding of the world is essentially the religious tradition of the *revealed religion*. Christian faith imbues the whole tradition of philosophy with its character of prejudice.[27] Modern philosophy sees tradition not as the source of truth but as the prejudice that enslaves human beings to the divine and to an understanding of nature as ordered by the divine. Modern philosophy founds itself in its forgetfulness of the tradition. Montaigne's "science of forgetfulness" (VS494, F365) is his ongoing liberation of the philosopher from his enslavement to divine revelation, tradition, and nature.

For Montaigne, we do not see nature as it really is but only through the distorting lens of tradition. Sacred tradition embodies a certain understanding of nature and man's place within nature. To engage in philosophy within the tradition is to accept the tradition's understanding of nature and to accept nature as unchangeable. To break free of the tradition is to break free of nature as the tradition understands it.

How does Montaigne free himself from the tradition? First, he reduces tradition to mere custom. Tradition has divine authority, whereas custom is a merely accidental human invention. The reduction of tradition to custom allows him to free himself from the divine authority of tradition and from submission to divine revelation.

Montaigne never addresses the tradition directly in the *Essays*. He uses the term "tradition" only once, and that single reference is not to sacred tradition but to the "tradition of the arts" (VS505, F374). While he never discusses sacred tradition, he does often talk about the great variety of human custom, a variety that has the effect of loosening the hold of custom on our belief. So, for example, in reply to those who claim that Christian faith is brought about in the believer "by a particular inspiration of divine grace" (VS440, F321), he argues that we are Christians because we happen to have been born in a country where Christianity was in practice. "We are Christians by the same title that we are Perigordians or Germans" (VS445, F325). He looks at faith not as a participant in the practice of faith but as a detached observer of the variety of religious custom.

Not only does he reduce tradition to custom; he reduces nature itself to custom. In spite of its merely accidental origin, custom has great power over us. "Custom is a violent and treacherous schoolmistress. She establishes in us, little by little, stealthily, the foothold of her authority; but having by this mild and humble beginning settled and planted it with the help of time, she soon uncovers to us a furious and tyrannical face against which we no longer have the liberty of even raising our eyes. We see her at every turn forcing the rules of nature" (VS109, F77). Even "the laws of conscience, which we say are born of nature, are born of custom" (VS115, F83). Custom exercises violence and force over our minds, an enslavement that is complete because we do not even recognize it. By reducing sacred tradition to custom, Montaigne undermines the authority of tradition by undermining its divine origin and showing it to be merely arbitrary and without a solid foundation. By reducing nature to custom, he shows nature to be changeable and malleable.

In "Of Custom" Montaigne tells us that he was once asked to defend a certain custom that was received with great authority in his culture. He wanted to establish this custom not as is usually done, by appeal to its persistence over time, but by "tracking it to its origin." Instead of discovering a solid foundation, he says: "I there found its foundation so weak that I nearly became disgusted with it" (VS116–17, F84).

It is here that we begin to see the emergence of philosophical self-consciousness. Montaigne says: "The principal effect of the power of custom is to seize and ensnare us in such a way that it is hardly within our power to get ourselves back out of its grip and *return to ourselves to reflect and reason* about its ordinances" (VS115, F83, emphasis added). In spite of its hold on us, it is possible to get out from under this power of custom. "Whoever wants to *essay himself* . . . and get rid of this violent prejudice of custom will find many things accepted with undoubting resolution, which have no support but in the hoary beard and the wrinkles of the usage that goes with them; but when this mask is torn off, and he refers things to truth and reason, he will feel his judgment as it were all upset, and nevertheless restored to a much surer status" (VS117, F84–85, emphasis added).[28]

When Montaigne tears off the mask of custom, his judgment is first upset because he has become distanced from the tradition, seeing it as arbitrary and weak. He no longer stands within the tradition as a believing participant. This is the skeptical moment of complete uncertainty. The reduction of the tradition to custom shows that he realizes that his mind was dominated by something foreign to itself. But it is also *the moment in which the mind shows itself,* for the mind itself has been suddenly called into question. When the mask is torn away, *reflection* occurs because the mind had been unselfconsciously looking at itself in the grip of tradition and now suddenly sees *itself,* unmasked. In that instant, the

mind catches a glimpse of itself, becomes transparent to itself and conscious of itself, conscious of itself as acting, coming into being through
its own agency. The mind of the philosopher is not "there" in the world
to be discovered in and through its relationship to the world but only
exists when it is brought into being, brings itself into being, in the act of
reflection. Reflection is always the mind returning to itself. It is this
notion of reflection that captures the meaning of philosophical self-
consciousness in the modern philosophical act. Modern philosophy
brings itself into being in this self-conscious reflection.

Montaigne "doubles himself and becomes the *spectator* of his own
mind."[29] His most explicit description of the act of reflection is found in
"Of Practice," where he tells us that he studies only himself and that his
task is to observe and follow the wandering movement of his mind and
to identify the innumerable flutterings that agitate it. He calls this "a new
and extraordinary amusement" and, at the same time, a very difficult and
useful work of description (VS378, F273). The mind's "principal and most
laborious study is studying itself" (VS819, F621).

Montaigne is following the "wanderings" and "flutterings" of the
mind. The essays themselves are perfect examples of the way he confronts
this wandering and fluttering of the mind: they are characterized by di-
gressions, accidental connections, and the apparent disorder of his
thought. He is not attempting to give an account of the "nature" of the
various aspects of his thought, but rather to observe the movement of his
thoughts. That the mind "wanders" shows that it has no naturally given
direction or end. To insist that his study means to "describe" himself
shows that he is not attempting to understand thought from the inside,
from the experience of the agent, as if it had a direction that would make
sense of it, but that he is watching from the "outside," catching the mind
unawares. The natural mind, then, is being brought under the control
of the philosophical mind. This is the act of reflection that the essays
display.

The mind of the philosopher is the mind that has no memory. Montaigne says: "There is no man who has less business talking about memory.
For I recognize almost no trace of it in me, and I do not think there is another one in the world so monstrously deficient. All my other faculties
are low and common; but in this one I think I am singular and very rare,

and thereby worthy of gaining a name and reputation" (VS34, F21). His forgetfulness of the tradition means that he sees everything *as if* for the first time. The doubleness, the reflexivity, of the mind is captured in the "as if" stance, for he does really know that what he is looking at is familiar and that he is not in fact seeing it for the first time. He knows that he does not know. Everything is new to him. Memory ties the mind to the eternal through the divine transmission of the tradition. Forgetfulness is the mind immersed in the temporal, always on the edge of the new, always open to the new. Forgetfulness is the mind without presuppositions.

The meaning of reflection is captured in the mind's attitude of "detachment" and "spying." Montaigne describes himself as *detached* from himself: "I dare not only to speak of myself, but to speak only of myself; I go astray when I write of anything else, and get away from my subject. I do not love myself so indiscriminately, nor am I so attached and wedded to myself, that I cannot distinguish and consider myself apart, as I do a neighbor or a tree" (VS942, F720). His detachment allows him to *spy* on himself: "Each man is a good education to himself, provided he has the capacity to spy on himself from close up" (VS377, F272).

Montaigne's detachment from himself means that he separates himself as the philosopher from himself as the natural man. He doubles himself, as it were.[30] Montaigne becomes as unknown to himself as a rock or a tree or another man. He has forgotten himself as formed by the tradition and must spy on himself so that he can catch himself unawares to see what his nature, freed from tradition, really is. He spies on the movements of his soul as if he, the philosopher, is not the originator or initiator of those actions. When it forgets the tradition, the mind sees itself as it is "in itself." Detachment and spying, then, are not the natural attitude of naïve, unselfconscious "introspection," but rather the nonnatural stance of modern philosophy in the self-conscious act of reflection.

One of the clearest examples of detachment and spying occurs in "Of Practice," where Montaigne recounts the incident in which he came so close to death that he was shown "the face and the *idea* of death" (VS373, F269, emphasis added). In a violent collision with a large and powerful horse, he had been thrown from his own horse and was unconscious, bleeding, and almost dead. His description of his return to consciousness presents him as if he were hovering over himself, watching himself, observing his faculties reawaken. It is here that he tells us that each man is a good education to himself, provided he has the capacity to spy on himself from close up. Pierre Manent explains Montaigne's doubling of himself in this incident: the agent in Montaigne was "deactivated" and made available for "objective knowledge." This kind of objective knowledge is "a new science, the *science of the subject*." The stance that Montaigne displays here is that of the "disengaged spectator."[31]

How, precisely, is Montaigne's new stance of detachment and spying achieved? How is this break with the natural traditional attitude possible? In "Of Presumption" Montaigne says that the only thing he esteems himself for is just what every man esteems himself for: "My recommendation is vulgar, common, and popular, for who ever thought he lacked sense?" We recognize the superiority of others in courage, strength, and beauty, "but an advantage in judgment we yield to no one" (VS656, F498). This presumption that our own judgments are true is universal, so Montaigne, then, is just like every other man. But here he does offer a way in which he can guarantee the uniqueness and the soundness of his opinions: "I think my opinions are good and sound; but who does not think as much of his? One of the best proofs I have of mine is the little esteem I have for myself" (VS657, F499). His lack of self-esteem is a new kind of proof: not the proof of logical demonstration, but proof based on the removal of the bias of self-esteem.

To be the detached observer, the philosopher must not see himself as he *wants* to be or as he wants to be seen as a participant in the order of nature. Montaigne says: "I who spy on myself more closely, who have my eyes unceasingly intent on myself, as one who has not much business elsewhere—I would hardly dare tell of the vanity and weakness that I find in myself" (VS565, F425). Because he has removed philosophy from the natural man, the natural man is weak. The fact that, when he becomes the invisible observer, he reveals the vanity and weakness of the natural man shows that his self-esteem, his will to recognition, and his pride are no longer present in his vision of himself as the man. This detachment from himself overcomes his natural philosophical presumption at the deepest level. That he must reject self-esteem shows that he is rejecting the tradition, the traditional place of philosophy in the hierarchy of nature.

When the mind forgets itself as formed by the tradition, it becomes conscious of itself as the origin of philosophy, its own act. There are not two minds now (the natural and the philosophical), but one mind that has forgotten itself and then discovers itself, the self-conscious mind. This is the mind that is in the man who happens to be the philosopher, the accidental philosopher.

We catch a glimpse of the hidden philosopher only in this *action* of the mind, freeing himself from tradition and emerging as something new. We catch a glimpse of him in the act of becoming, the coming into being of the modern philosophical mind. "Philosophy becomes the self-generation of the mind as something that is not given by nature."[32] At the same time that the mind frees itself from nature, it generates *itself*, brings itself into being. This is modern philosophy founding itself.

The traditional philosopher loses himself and forgets himself in the contemplation of Being. Montaigne turns back from Being to himself in the act of reflection. He loses himself and forgets himself as the natural man and discovers himself as the philosopher, becomes conscious of himself as the philosopher. Discovering himself as the philosopher is astonishing to him. But at the same time, he has made himself to be what he is: this is his freedom, his own act, the act of becoming self-conscious.

Now we can begin to see why the modern philosopher must turn to himself in order to take the stance of the detached observer and why the philosophical act ends in astonishment. We can see the sleight of hand in which the traditional philosopher is replaced by the modern philosopher who seizes power over nature.

First, why must he turn to himself? In "Of Experience" Montaigne writes: "I study myself more than any other subject. That is my metaphysics, that is my physics" (VS1072, F821). The subject matter of metaphysics was traditionally Being as such, eternal and unchanging; the subject matter of physics was traditionally the natural world. For Montaigne, traditional metaphysics and physics have both been pursued in the mode of the presumption of the philosopher—namely, that the philosopher is within the world of nature and that he participates in the divine.

Only one man can break free of that presumption of the philosopher for the first time. Only a particular man can become two, separate himself as the philosopher from the natural man, from the human species, and thus separate philosophy from nature for the first time. Only one man can make this move because the new philosophical act is not the actualization of a potentiality given to human nature as such. It is rather a possibility invented and brought into being by the particular man who doubles himself.

Only the particular man can double himself and take the stance of the objective observer, yet the observer must have within himself nothing of the particularity of the man. His own private will, especially his own private will to recognition, is not present in the observer. In order to become the observer, he must surrender his particularity as a man. He must hide himself as the observer and surrender his being and his place in the natural hierarchy. The traditional philosopher must not only disappear; he must empty himself of himself.

The requirement of the self-effacement of the philosopher helps us to make sense of one of the strangest passages in the *Essays*. In his discussion of the motives for suicide, Montaigne mentions first the desire to escape the evils of this world. But, as usual, he offers another possible cause: "Men also sometimes desire death in the hope of a greater good." Then, as he frequently does, he points to a Christian and a pagan example: "'I desire,' says Saint Paul, 'to be dissolved, to be with Jesus Christ.'" And Cleombrotus of Ambracia threw himself into the sea because his reading of Plato's *Phaedo* had given him such a strong desire for the life to come. Montaigne, however, is a third type: "Whence it appears how improperly we call 'despair' that voluntary dissolution to which we are often borne by the ardor of hope, and often by a tranquil and deliberate inclination of our judgment" (VS360, F260). This third type of voluntary dissolution of the self, this tranquil and deliberate inclination of judgment, refers, I believe, to Montaigne's own self-effacement, the self-effacement of the traditional philosopher for "a greater good." Montaigne has to turn to himself so that he can efface himself, and this act of self-effacement is the invisible power that brings the new order into being.

Second, why does the philosophical act end in astonishment at what he himself has produced? In the first moment of the philosophical act, Montaigne separates the detached observer from the natural man and becomes "double" within himself so that, as the philosopher, he can spy on himself and catch himself, the natural man, unawares. The act of detachment and spying, this doubling of himself, is an action in which "the left hand does not know what the right hand is doing." This expression comes from the Gospel of Matthew: "When you give alms, your left hand must not know what your right hand is doing; your almsgiving must be secret, and your Father who sees all that is done in secret will reward you."[33] The action must be secret not only from other people but also, in some way, from the agent himself.

The doubleness of "the left hand not knowing what the right hand is doing" comes through in a strange story that Montaigne tells about himself and an unidentified friend. Commentators have speculated that, in at least one instance in this essay, when Montaigne refers to an unnamed friend, he is really referring to himself, in the way that one might attribute to an imagined friend something about oneself that one would not want to reveal directly. I believe this is the case in the story under consideration.

His friend is afraid that a supernatural "enchantment" has been placed on him by a rival to make him impotent on his wedding night. Montaigne assures him that he has "a counterbattery of enchantments" (VS100, F70) at his disposal to save his friend from this disaster. Montaigne waits, hidden outside the door of the wedding chamber, and when his friend signals that the dreaded, humiliating, and shameful powerlessness has come upon him, Montaigne gives him a medal engraved with celestial figures to tie around his waist. Miraculously, the impotence is overcome! Montaigne tells us that he himself does not believe in miracles and supernatural enchantments, but this counterenchantment, he says, is "a miracle which was in my power" (VS100, F71).

Montaigne has doubled himself as the observer and the natural man: the story shows us the observer who does not believe in enchantments and the natural man who is made powerful through a deception of which he knows nothing. What the observer brings is freedom from belief in the supernatural. But he uses the deception of celestial power to free the man from the power of the supernatural. In what is the only instance of such a confession in the *Essays*, Montaigne writes: "It was a sudden and curious whim that led me to do such a thing, which was alien to my nature. I am an enemy of subtle and dissimulated acts and hate trickery in myself, not only for sport but also for someone's profit. If the action is not vicious, the road to it is" (VS101, F71). This is the sleight of hand, the trick of the mind, that takes away the paralyzing fear of the supernatural and produces the astonishing miracle that allows the human being to exercise his own power. And where does the power of man, the human, show itself more literally than in the power of the sexual act to generate the new human being out of itself?

The hidden, detached observer is revealed in the becoming of the man. Montaigne is astonished to see that his weak thoughts and mores conform by accident to so many of the teachings of ancient philosophy. He uses the language of "astonishment" rather than the traditional philosophical term "wonder." Ancient philosophy begins in wonder. Wonder implies something given, something mysterious. We do not wonder at what we ourselves have made, because we already know what has gone into it and how it was produced. Montaigne does not wonder at what he has produced, because he himself has produced it and he knows that he has produced it, but he is astonished at what he has produced because he did not know what he was doing. (The left hand did not know what the right hand was doing.) That is why he refers to himself as an "unpremeditated" philosopher: it is as if he says the first words that come to his mouth, without knowing what he is going to say.

Montaigne could not have that experience of astonishment if he knew what he was doing. He is astonished at what he himself has brought forth because there is nothing of himself in it: it is without his own private will. He must not know what he was doing, because it cannot be merely his own private will that is being satisfied in the philosophical act. What he brings forth must emerge spontaneously from the philosophical act itself, thus from human freedom. This is an act that seems to simply "pass through" him, as if he is merely the channel.[34] Therefore, there is a sense in which he does not produce what he (the natural man) *wants* to produce, but what must be produced out of the philosophical act. The action simply passes through him, because he has become the channel of the pure human will. That is, it is not his own private will that is expressed in what he becomes but rather a will that is without any particularity.

Montaigne cannot remember the interval between his desire to reveal himself and the actual revelation of himself, because that interval is his self-effacement. He has to forget himself as his natural mind in order to become conscious of himself as the philosophical mind. The mind dominated by the tradition has to be forgotten in order to be completely erased. Yet what he has forgotten, his forgetting, is always there in the consciousness of doubleness. His own act is *experienced* not as something he did but as something that happened to him (passed through him). It is "as if" philosophy becomes conscious of *itself* in him. He is (merely) an unpremeditated and accidental philosopher, the man who happens to be the philosopher, in whom and through whom philosophy becomes conscious of itself.[35]

Philosophical reflection originates in the philosopher's dissatisfaction with human nature and in his shame for the ineffectiveness of philosophy in settling the conflict between masters and slaves, strong and weak. Gerhard Kruger explains: "Reflection in the fundamental, philosophical sense of the word, man's 'reflectivity,' presupposes *the powerlessness of man before God*, as it is understood by Christianity."[36] Therefore, "self-consciousness forms itself *in defiance of* all divine omnipotence: . . . [thus] here begins the philosophical revolt against Christianity that we call the *Aufklärung*."[37]

Montaigne, then, sees God as the omnipotent master, and in relation to this omnipotent master, we are all slaves. Reflection originates in dissatisfaction and shame over our powerlessness: reflection is rebellion against God's omnipotence, and this rebellion is human freedom. Montaigne subjects Christianity to philosophy: hence, the "ineffable" character of the detached observer and the astonishment at what has simply "happened" to him "as if" it were the action of divine grace. The detached observer replaces "the Father who sees in secret." This is the rebellion of original sin: that man can do this himself, that through the sleight-of-hand of the philosopher's self-effacement, the natural human self can be annihilated, not by divine grace but by the human will.

The New Adam

Montaigne is the new Adam, the first man, the new man, not created by God, but brought into being by his own power. The being who appears before us in the *Essays* reveals himself as "double." He is the union of the detached observer and the natural animal. The original "human" has disappeared. That is why Montaigne describes himself as a monster and a miracle: "I have seen no more evident monstrosity and miracle in the world than myself" (VS1029, F787). Man is now "the subject," and "the subject is this animal-divine."[38]

The so-called mind-body problem of modern philosophy is not about a distinction within the natural man. In Aristotle's account of philosophy and the theoretical sciences in general, all human knowledge begins in the senses and proceeds through memory and experience to the arts and finally the sciences. There is a harmony and continuity between the intellect and the body in which the intellect receives from the senses, memory, and imagination the material for the apprehension of the form of the object of knowledge. The intellect depends upon the body, the senses, and the imagination. The soul is the "form" of the body and is not separable from the body. The traditional definition of man as "the rational animal" means that man is an animal who is rational. There is no "mind-body problem" for ancient philosophy. But there is a problem for modern philosophy because the "mind" is not the natural mind but the detached, nonnatural philosophical mind, which is somehow tied to a body, an animal.[39]

Montaigne's stance, then, is very different from the stance of Aristotelian philosophy. The philosopher in the natural attitude sees where the species fits into the hierarchy of nature and where the philosopher fits into the species. In taking this approach, the philosopher does not separate himself from the natural man. The classical philosopher remains a participant in nature: his own activity is natural, the highest fulfillment and perfection of human nature. Indeed, for Aristotle, philosophy is divine, a participation in the divine activity of thought thinking thought. Philosophy orders the traditional hierarchy by its participation in nature.

Montaigne's new objective stance is the separation of the philosopher from the natural man. Because he has become the observer, he is no longer a participant, as the philosopher, in the natural hierarchy. Therefore, the hierarchy within human nature is destroyed by this simple act of taking the detached observer's stance. Whereas the classical philosopher orders the hierarchy by participating in it as the highest, Montaigne destroys the hierarchy by becoming the observer who does not participate.

By removing himself as a participant in nature, the philosopher *transforms* nature. And "it is by the transformation of nature that man takes full possession of his capacity to transform himself."[40]

The second moment of the philosophical act, then, is the act of invention, of judging and thus reordering the fragments of the shattered traditional hierarchy. Montaigne says that the essays are the "tests" (*essais*) of his judgment (VS301, F219; VS653, F495). Philosophical invention occurs in the act of judgment. The modern philosophical mind comes into being as judgment because judgment is the self-conscious act of mastering, subjecting, and reordering human nature. Judgment makes the philosophical act effective: it effects, brings into being, the new man, because it reunites the detached observer and the natural man.

When the detached observer is separated from the natural man, nature itself is changed, because it is now without philosophy as the natural activity that orders the nature of the human being. The natural hierarchy collapses, and the philosopher, removed from the hierarchy, stands before the pieces, which are now in no essential order. The natural human being is no longer a "form" directed to an "end," but a collection of accidents ordered to no naturally given end. When the mind is taken out of nature, nature, and human nature in particular, becomes just the "matter" on which the philosopher can impose any form he wants. The sensations, images, passions, and feelings that happen to him, that he undergoes, are treated as mere accidents to be accepted, rejected, combined, or separated according to the will of the philosopher. The natural direction of the human being to the good is replaced by the power of the will to impose its own chosen form and direction on the fragments of human nature.

In other words, the good is removed from nature and located in the choices of the human will. Since nature can give him no guidance, the philosopher must decide how the fragments are to be ordered. This moment of freedom is the moment of complete indeterminateness, the moment of the freedom of the philosopher to impose a new order upon human beings and the human world. He stands now in a relationship to nature of mastery and judgment, not of participation and contemplation.

It may be helpful to consider the way in which detachment, spying, invention, and judgment are practiced in modern science in order to better understand the stance and the action of the detached observer in the *Essays*. The modern philosophical act makes modern science possible. The philosopher performs the most fundamental and most difficult act, the original act of detachment of the mind from nature. Modern natural science, the social sciences, and empirical psychology are all manifestations of the detached observer. They require the scientist to abandon the natural attitude toward the world and to adopt the stance of the mind that is not a part of nature. The natural mind—its sensations and imaginations—is submitted to the "method" that allows nature to reveal itself in the ways appropriate for its domination by man.

The modern scientist does not see nature as a world of unchangeable forms and naturally given ends. That is the fundamental prejudice that he must put aside. Nature is a world of accidents in no essential order. The modern scientist does not want to simply understand nature: he seeks to discover some new possibility that can be produced by separating and combining certain qualities that are not found separated or combined in natural things. (For example, he might want to find a treatment that would make wood fireproof.) In order to do that he must suspend his presuppositions and be open to the unexpected. With the history of past attempts in mind, he imagines or invents hypotheses that he can test in his laboratory.

The detachment of the modern scientist can be understood in the idea of the scientific "experiment." The experiment introduces a new level of distance, of separation, between the mind and the experience we have of the world in our everyday encounters with it. As Francis Bacon explains, "Simple experience . . . , if taken as it comes, is called accident; if it is deliberately sought, it is called experiment."[41] The experiment is a "deliberately sought" experience, a highly structured and controlled event of observation in which things are combined and separated in ways that do not occur in the world in order to see what happens and to allow something new to emerge. The scientist uses his imagination to invent and then test his hypotheses, showing that his concern is with what might happen, what he might be able to bring about in the experiment.

The purpose of modern science is not the Aristotelian natural end of knowledge for its own sake but the subjection of nature and of human being to the will of man. And this requires a method that does not allow the mind to simply follow its own natural course. As Bacon says, "The whole operation of the mind must be completely re-started, so that from the very beginning it is not left to itself, but is always subject to rule."[42] In this way, the mind can exercise its "rightful authority over the nature of things."[43] The detached observer is the scientific mind that rules over the natural mind, directing the senses and the imagination in its inquiries into nature.

We can consider Montaigne's *Essays* as experiments: indeed, he may have chosen this title in order to suggest that meaning. One meaning of the term "essay" is "trial" or "test." The *Essays* are the trials and tests of the natural mind, the "deliberately sought" experience of the natural mind by the detached observer, the natural mind put to the test by the detached observer. Montaigne performs what had seemed to be the impossible task of the mind looking at itself and ruling itself. To "deliberately seek" an experience of the natural mind is to double the mind, bringing the detached observer into being. In the *Essays* we are catching a glimpse of the detached observer coming into being in the stance that Montaigne takes on himself.

Like the natural scientist, he sees human nature as a disordered collection of accidents, not as an unchangeable form directed to a naturally given end. Having overcome that fundamental prejudice, Montaigne "catches himself unawares" in the experiments of the essays. We can examine the first essay, "By Diverse Means We Arrive at the Same End," as an example of the "method" Montaigne uses to spy on himself. In the space of only three pages, he tells eight stories about conquering princes taken from both ancient histories and contemporary sources, without regard to chronological order. If he is intent upon studying only himself, why does he bring before the mind these many stories about other men? He does this because he cannot begin by looking directly at himself. This is not naïve, natural introspection. He has to be revealed to himself indirectly, catching himself unawares. He must appear to himself suddenly in his newness, his uniqueness, and originality. That is, he must forget his old self in order to discover his new particularity. The stories he recounts are "instances" of human behavior recounted in the histories. History, he says, is "the skeleton of philosophy," in which the most abstruse aspects of human behavior can be observed (VS156, F115).

The way he approaches the histories reveals his true purpose. The historians are at least one step removed from the actual event, so he is really beginning from the historian's account, which, in turn, is probably based on hearsay. When he considers the histories, he goes further and invents the character traits of the historical figures: he "probes the inside," uncovering the "springs of action" (VS338, F244). In other words, he finds "intimations" of his new character in the great philosophers and princes of the past. Montaigne says that, because he is concerned with "what can happen," not with what has happened, fabulous testimonies are just as useful for him as accurate testimonies, because they reveal some human possibility (VS105–6, F75). He is interested in what is possible for human beings to do, but more fundamentally, in what human beings are capable of believing, because he is intent on reforming the most basic prejudices of the natural mind. Therefore, in addition to historical examples, he examines all kinds of opinion, both common opinions and philosophical teachings and mores.

In this first essay, Montaigne compares the actions and motivations of princes and ordinary people, finding similarities and differences and following the flow of his thought through the accidental similarities that link very different kinds of human beings. In this way, he overturns our presuppositions about strong and weak "natures" by discovering surprising similarities between strong and weak. This approach of examining a wide variety of instances, seeking out accidental similarities across different kinds of "natures," "probing the inside," and combining qualities in new ways is the approach of modern science to the objects of its investigations.

Montaigne discovers to his astonishment that he is a new figure of the philosopher. What is revealed to Montaigne about himself and what surprises him in the experiment of the first essay is his own "marvelous weakness in the direction of mercy and gentleness" (VS8, F4). Unlike the Stoic philosophers, he is easily moved to pity. From the fragments of the stories of princes and peoples, from common opinions and the teachings of philosophers, the detached observer has invented and uncovered the possibility of a new kind of philosopher, the philosopher who feels pity, the mind of the detached observer reunited with the animal, natural man.

The first essay is his first attempt at uncovering and destroying the most deeply held prejudice of the natural mind, the prejudice in favor of the strong that is the foundation of the traditional hierarchy of strong and weak. He tears away the mask of the traditional understanding of man and penetrates to a very different understanding. The destruction of this prejudice allows the new Adam to emerge. Montaigne catches himself unawares in the experiments of the essays, discovering his new character and building his foundation for the reformation of human nature and the resolution of the conflict between masters and slaves that is his philosophical project.

The new philosophical act of judgment overcomes the classical distinction between actions that are for their own sake and actions that are for the sake of producing something other than the act itself.[44] Unlike contemplation, judgment produces an effect, the new order, but unlike the effect of the act of production, the effect of judgment is not different from the act that produces it. In other words, *judgment itself is the new order, the new relationship between mind and being.* Judgment, as Montaigne understands it, is the reversal of the natural relationship between the mind and being in which the mind is measured by being. Being is now subject to the human mind. Judgment is a new possibility of thought, for, unlike the natural act of contemplation, judgment includes an act of the will. It is the act in which the mind frees itself from nature and subjects nature to the human will.

Montaigne's sleight of hand changes the traditional standard of judgment. For Aristotle, the particular is subsumed and judged under the standard of the universal. The standard of judgment is what should be: you cannot see what something is (in its incompleteness and imperfection) unless you see it from the standpoint of what it should be, the standard and measure of the best, the standard of form and final cause, of completion and perfection. For Montaigne, however, the standard of judgment is not what *should* be but what *could* be. He does not subsume the particular under the universal. Montaigne looks at what is, not in the light of what it should be by nature, but in terms of how it could be formed by the philosopher to bring forth something new.

Judgment invents the new self-creating individual: one's judgment is one's individuality. In his essay on the education of children, Montaigne works out the distinction between mere learning and true education in terms of the difference between simply borrowing from the ancients, which is only an exercise of memory, and forming one's own judgment. When he describes education as a mere exercise of memory, he means that education has always been simply about absorbing the tradition, submitting one's mind to the tradition. Forming one's own judgment, on the other hand, is a very different understanding of what education should be. The student should be taught what to do with the pieces, the fragments, borrowed from others: "He will transform and blend them to make a work that is all his own, [that is], his judgment. His education, work, and study aim only at forming this" (VS152, F111). The bringing into being of the mind as judgment is precisely this act of forming his judgment, which is "a work all his own." Judgment is the mind taking possession of itself, directing itself.

Judgment, philosophical invention, is what happens when the mind looks at what is presented and given to it as material for what it can bring into being. Judgment looks at the contents of the mind in light of what it *wants*. What it wants is not man as he is but a new man. That new man has to be invented by the mind itself. It cannot come simply from the materials that are presented and given: the materials have to be ordered according to what the philosophical mind wills.

Judgment, then, is not about "what is" but about what is possible. Montaigne says that "there are authors whose end is to tell what has happened. *Mine*, if I could attain it, would be to talk about what *can* happen" (VS105–6, F75, emphasis added). The "end" is "mine," not the naturally given universal end of all human beings, but his own purpose and project, which he may or may not be able to attain: the end is a possibility. "What is" is reduced to merely "what has been"; eternal Being becomes merely what has happened in the past, so that the mind is opened to the new. Becoming, without a naturally given end, becomes not the actualization of potentiality but the bringing into being of the possible. The essays are the tests of his judgment, because he is testing the possible, testing what can be brought out of the old, out of the tradition.

The Aristotelian metaphysics of form and final cause, potentiality and actuality, does not allow for the coming into being of the genuinely new, because becoming is always simply actualization of potentialities given by nature and belonging to the species. The genuinely new can emerge only as the possible. Potentialities and actualities are given by nature; possibilities are not given by nature but are invented and made real by the mind freed from the constraints of nature: they do not become actual unless the mind effects them.

On the one hand, then, what Montaigne wants to produce *is already there*, in the old, in the fragments of the tradition. On the other hand, the new *is not already there*. Montaigne always speaks as if he is simply discovering something in nature that was always already there, but it is really produced by himself. Montaigne "discovers" in ancient philosophy and in Christianity the new thoughts and mores that he himself invents. That is why, although his essays are about himself and only himself, so many philosophers, historians, poets, theologians, saints, and princes make an appearance. When he looks back at the classical-Christian tradition, he finds "intimations" of the new man. Intimations are hints, glimpses, of something not yet self-conscious. Intimations are possibilities that depend upon the philosopher to be brought out and made self-conscious. It is as if the entire history of classical-Christian civilization becomes conscious of itself in him, in this particular man.

Philosophical invention brings the new out of the old by reordering the pieces of the shattered tradition. This is the new human nature of which he is the origin. The moment of complete indeterminateness in the philosophical act is the moment of human action, the moment of freedom and possibility. Freedom in the modern world is freedom from naturally given ends and therefore freedom from nature. Montaigne frees action itself from the natural constraint of final cause. Action is now a beginning, without an end, having no natural direction. Action without natural direction is power. The philosophical act is the invisible power that produces the effect, the new order. This is the moment in which action *is* thought, not of what is given, not receptive, but originative: the moment of bringing the new out of the mind itself. Judgment discovers truth only in the sense that it invents truth, brings truth into being because it brings the possible into being. In the words of Machiavelli, this is the "effectual" truth.[45]

Montaigne's "end," then, is not the naturally given end of contemplation, for it is his freely chosen purpose. *It is not a fixed state, not a state of completion (such as contemplation is), for there can be no such fixed state, no such completion.* Rather, philosophical invention or judgment is the stance of openness to the possible, an ongoing condition of freedom in relation to the past and the future. Therefore, judgment is, in a way, above the order of time, above immersion in the temporal. Yet it is not the eternal stance of ancient philosophy. Montaigne is always at the edge of coming into being. This is the order of Becoming as such, replacing the ancient order of Being as such.[46] *This* is Montaigne's new philosophical stance, the strange new place in which he stands to essay himself. The "essay" is an experiment, a try or trial of what it is possible for the mind to bring into being.

Philosophy, then, is no longer leisure. Philosophical invention is play and work. When Montaigne sets out the meaning of reflection and the way he spies on his own mind, he refers to this activity of reflection as "a new and extraordinary amusement" and, at the same time, as an act of the greatest "difficulty" and "usefulness." Philosophy is play because it is the mind's endless play with possibility. It is work because it is the endless toil of bringing the new into being. Man is now complete in himself not because he has attained the naturally given end of perfection but because, through self-consciousness, he is ordered to himself and takes possession of himself.

Montaigne, then, has moved from dissatisfaction to satisfaction and from shame at his powerlessness to the power of invention. He has *become* a new man and he has done this through his own power. That is his satisfaction: bringing the new man into being. Man is no longer the being who stands in wonder and awe before the created world and its Creator. He is now the self-creating being who, standing in astonishment at what he himself brings into being, declares it to be good.

In the following chapters, I set out the structure of the modern political and moral world invented by the philosopher, the world in which the new human being is at home. The new man is ordered not to God but to himself, and he lives not in the political community of the city but in the liberal order of state and society. His moral perfection, his greatness, is not heroic virtue but "authenticity," which Montaigne describes as "knowing how to belong to oneself" and as "the greatest thing in the world." This authentic individual is related to others not through his participation in the tradition but in terms of the new social bond of civility. However, the failure of civility and the disintegration of the social bond reveal that the natural human self is not annihilated but only suppressed and hidden in the sleight of hand of the modern philosophical act.

TWO

The New Order

Hidden Mastery

REORDERING MAN TO MAN

Montaigne often points to the danger, risk, and boldness of his project. The man who seeks to introduce change "must be very sure that he sees the weakness of what he is casting out and the goodness of what he is bringing in" (VS121, F88). The moment in which he must choose how to order man to man is the moment of greatest freedom and therefore the moment of greatest risk. As the detached observer, he removes himself as a participant in the moral world and suspends his judgment about good and evil. Everything within the tradition is called into question and revalued, submitted to the judgment of the philosopher. This is possible only through philosophical reflection because that is the only way that man can "get outside" his traditional assumptions to look at them and evaluate them.[1] Reflection is the action of the mind looking at itself, considering itself. To get beneath our most deeply held presuppositions is to seek the conditions that explain why we think what we think, to put aside all presuppositions about good and evil and to ask simply why we see things this way.

The presupposition that Montaigne wants to understand in its underlying presumption is the natural hierarchy that justifies the master-slave relationship. Why do we accept this hierarchy and this relationship? The understanding that he gains in the act of reflection is that the condition for this natural understanding is the preference that we have for the difficult, rare, extraordinary, and strong over the easy, common, ordinary, and weak. It is this deeply rooted natural hierarchical preference or *prejudice* that must be overcome if man is to order himself to himself.

The fundamental meaning of the replacement of contemplation by judgment is that value or ranking now comes from man himself. Judgment is the act of weighing, evaluating, and ordering. This is the reversal of the traditional order, in which "the good in itself and for its own sake" is given by nature. Nature can no longer give us guidance, because, on account of the destruction of the hierarchy, it is no longer the standard of worth. When he speaks about "worth," Montaigne moves between the language of "the good," even "the good for its own sake," and the language of "value," thus conflating these two very different meanings.[2] Values are relative to the human will; the good "in itself" is not. Montaigne's project is the revaluation of all things in relation to the human will.

Rémi Brague explains the idea of "value" in relation to the modern notion of subjectivity: "The idea of value implies the entrance of the good into the orbit of subjectivity. . . . An important step toward the entrance of the idea of value into the orbit of subjectivity is already found in Montaigne." The shift to the idea of value means that "the good no longer is directly worthwhile, as good, but rather as what has value. It no longer derives its goodness from itself, but from the value assigned to it. . . . It is the subject and his power of valorization which then becomes the supreme value. The subjection of the idea of the good to that of value thus shows itself to be but one more expression of the sovereignty of the modern subject."[3]

Whereas the natural hierarchy is constituted by the direction of man to the divine and thus rests upon what is highest in man, there is now nothing in the shattered tradition to help the philosopher determine how to direct man to man or how to rank the fragments that confront him. How does he know what the good of man is without an "external" standard, without the standard of something higher than man? If the hierarchy has been destroyed, how can anything be better than anything else?

The only guide that Montaigne has is the purity of his judgment, which makes him the channel of the pure human will. Because Montaigne's judgment has been purified of his particularity as a man, of the desires of his particular will, he can evaluate and redirect the fragments of human nature to their true end, the human good. That is, the philosopher does not discover the good in nature but brings it into being by his revaluation.

According to the tradition, the human is valued in relation to the divine, for the human is fulfilled, completed, and perfected only in union with the divine. Therefore, the standard of man simply as man looks like imperfection from the perspective of the tradition. Montaigne embraces this kind of imperfection and introduces a new kind of perfection. At the very end of the *Essays* he says: "It is an absolute perfection and God-like (*comme divine*) to know how to enjoy *our own being* rightly. We seek other conditions because we do not understand the use of our own, and go outside of ourselves because we do not know what it is like inside" (VS1115, F857, emphasis added).

Montaigne's destruction of the hierarchy is effected by his renunciation of self-esteem, and Montaigne can claim that his judgments are true because he has no self-esteem. But even though he does not esteem himself, he does love himself. In his revaluing of the human for its own sake, Montaigne demonstrates that the removal of esteem for the "highest" in man need not entail contempt for the human as such. The good of man as man requires this separation of self-esteem from self-love. Thus, in ordering man to man, Montaigne is inventing a new human nature in which self-love does not depend upon self-esteem.

First, he must overcome the contempt for the merely human that he sees in the old order. Montaigne repeatedly decries the contempt we have for ourselves for being merely human: "As for the opinion that disdains our life, it is ridiculous. For after all, life is our being, it is our all. . . . It is a malady peculiar to man, and not seen in any other creature, to hate and disdain himself" (VS353, F254). To despise our own being is "the most barbarous of our maladies" (VS1110, F852). The desire to rise above the human is the source of the greatest evils. Those who disdain the merely human, who want to be angels rather than men, "want to get out of themselves and escape from the man. That is madness: instead of changing into angels, they change into beasts; instead of raising themselves, they lower themselves. These transcendental humors frighten me" (VS1115, F856).

From the perspective of the traditional hierarchy, the ordering of man to man, the valuing of the human as such and for its own sake, looks like a "lowering" of the standard of the good. The "higher things" are difficult, rare, and extraordinary, rising above the merely human, which is common and ordinary. Therefore, self-esteem is tied to difficulty. Our natural presumption is that strength means preferring the difficult, the rare, and the extraordinary, that "difficulty gives value to things" (VS613, F464). But Montaigne says that "it is a marvelous testimony to *the weakness of our judgment* that it recommends things for their rarity or novelty, or even for their difficulty, even if they are neither good nor useful" (VS311, F226, emphasis added). In Montaigne's new order, the easy, the common, and the ordinary are more highly valued than the "higher things." To recognize this reversal of values, one must see ordinary human actions "in their proper light," the light of the good of man as man (VS1081, F829).

Montaigne's revaluation of human action can also be seen in his new ranking of the vices. In "Of Drunkenness," he claims that "our teachers" often rank sins badly; that is, the teaching of the tradition on the relative seriousness of vices is actually harmful. Drunkenness is "a gross and brutish vice," because it is "all bodily and earthy," and Montaigne finds it very distasteful. However, the course of his thinking in this essay leads him to conclude: "I find [drunkenness] a loose and stupid vice, but less malicious and harmful than the others, which almost all clash more directly with society in general." Drunkenness "costs our conscience less" than the vices that come from malice (VS342, F247). Vices that are bodily and earthy, such as drunkenness, gluttony, and lust, are more shameful in common opinion, but they are actually less evil than the vices such as envy, anger, and pride that have an intellectual component and are harmful to others. Rather than ranking the virtues and vices according to the classical standard of self-perfection and self-esteem, he ranks them according to the requirements of the new order.

What, then, is the good that Montaigne produces and how does he bring it about? The classical-Christian tradition had justified the hierarchy of masters and slaves insofar as that hierarchy depends upon the fundamental distinction between free and servile activities. It covered over the natural conflict between masters and slaves by the deception of the standard of the "common good" and the distinction between actions that are ends in themselves and actions that are for the sake of production, the distinction that justified the practice of slavery. The good that Montaigne seeks to bring into being is the resolution of the natural conflict between masters and slaves. He does this through the modern philosophical act itself, which eliminates the distinction between actions. Thus, he frees the slaves and "brings down" the masters. In the words of Machiavelli, he "eliminates the gentlemen." Montaigne frees the slaves by revaluing the most common and ordinary actions, which are regarded as "servile" within the tradition. Eliminating the gentlemen, however, is the greater problem, because the masters do not want to settle the conflict, for they value the honor of struggle and risk more highly than life itself. What is displayed in the *Essays*, then, is the revaluing of honor and the honorable. When the detached observer looks at the natural man, he sees that it is the "spirited" part of the soul (what the Greeks called *thumos*) that must be suppressed.

Montaigne says that weak and strong, masters and slaves are *by nature* at war with each other (VS918, F701). If the perpetual war of strong and weak is to be brought to an end, one man must be the first to lay down his arms, to take the greatest risk, by making himself more vulnerable, on the chance that the others will lay down their arms and settle for peace. Michael Oakeshott, in his discussion of how the social contract ever gets started in Hobbes's *Leviathan*, calls this act of submission the "moralization of pride" and refers explicitly to the character that appears in the *Essays*.

Hobbes relies on the fact that the greatest fear that most men experience is the fear of death. This fear drives them out of the state of nature and into the contract that is the commonwealth. But Hobbes recognizes that not all men can be ruled by the fear of death. The proud man would rather die than submit, would rather die than be forced to accept equality with the common men who do submit out of fear. In fact, according to Oakeshott, Hobbes actually needs such proud men, because they are more likely to make the first gesture toward peace. They are the ones who must be counted on to risk their lives by laying down their arms while the others retain theirs. This gesture comes not from fear but from a certain kind of generosity that can belong only to the proud. The proud achieve through courage what others achieve through rational calculation inspired by fear.

The man whose pride has been moralized is "a man whose disposition is to overcome fear not by reason (that is, by seeking a secure condition of external human circumstances) but by his own courage; a man not at all without imperfections and not deceived about himself, but who is proud enough to be spared the sorrow of his imperfections and the illusions of his achievements; not exactly a hero, too negligent for that, but perhaps with a touch of careless heroism about him; a man, in short, who (in Montaigne's phrase) 'knows how to belong to himself,' and who, if fortune turned out so, would feel no shame in the epitaph: 'Par delicatesse / J'ai perdu ma vie.'"[4]

Although, as Oakeshott maintains, Hobbes must presume upon the generosity of the proud, he constructs his commonwealth on the foundation of the fear of death that characterizes the weak. That is, the proud or spirited, who play such an important role in the state of nature, must disappear from his commonwealth. "If Nature therefore have made men equall, that equalitie is to be acknowledged: or if Nature have made men unequall; yet because men that think themselves equall, will not enter into conditions of Peace, but upon Equall termes, such equalitie must be admitted. And therefore for the ninth law of Nature, I put this, *That every man acknowledge [every] other for his Equall by Nature.* The breach of this Precept is *Pride*."[5]

In the natural conflict between strong and weak, masters and slaves, Montaigne is the first to lay down his arms. Laying down his "arms" is the disappearance of his strength and superiority as a philosopher. This self-effacement is the necessary condition for peace and for equality. The philosopher must be the first to lay down his arms, to surrender, because he holds the highest rank in the traditional hierarchy. One and only one man must act, but his act must look like mere submission motivated by fear of death. He risks his life, but only he knows it. He must be alone, for the motive for his action takes place entirely within himself: his strength must be invisible because it must be impossible to know from the outside that it is not weakness that moves him to be the first to lay down his arms.

His voluntary submission looks servile and weak, but his submission is really a free act, because it originates not in fear but in his own strength and generosity: he gets no recognition from it, because he disappears into the common and lowest, who submit out of weakness.

That the philosopher is actually reordering the fragments of the tradition must be hidden, because if philosophy appears as the origin of the new order, it simply reasserts its superiority, the superiority that had to disappear in order to destroy the old order. Not only does Montaigne perform this generous act that entails nothing less than his own self-effacement; he presents it, and he must present it, as easy and of no great value: "It does indeed seem to me that we overvalue [greatness], and overvalue too the resolution of people we have seen or heard of who despised it and laid it down of their own accord. . . . To eschew greatness is a virtue, it seems to me, which I, who am only a gosling, could attain without striving" (VS916, F699). Montaigne realizes the very difficult and risky nature of his project, but he hides that risk under the appearance of ease: "Nothing noble is done without risk" (VS129, F94). But "you can more easily dare what no one thinks you will dare, which becomes easy by its difficulty" (VS890, F679).

The strong show themselves in despising death, thus despising "mere" life, for the sake of something higher. Montaigne hides his strength. The strength of the great has to be turned into an internal, hidden act of strength, for it manifests itself *naturally* in the desire for the recognition that comes from the visible display of despising life itself in violent and noble deeds that risk one's life. Montaigne's submission is a *free* act, not because it is the attainment of a naturally given end in itself, but because it originates in his own will. At the same time, it is free and generous because he gets nothing out of it. He gets for himself no higher place in the visible hierarchy: he has mastered the natural desire for recognition and glory. He gets nothing from it *because* he disappears. That is what makes the act entirely good and entirely his own.

The "for its own sake" becomes the hiddenness and interiority of the moralization of pride. In "Of Husbanding One's Will," Montaigne discusses his own actions as mayor of Bordeaux, emphasizing the fact that he did not seek his own good or his own glory in carrying out the duties of that office. He writes: "Those actions have much more grace which escape from the hand of the workman nonchalantly and noiselessly, and which some worthy man later picks out and lifts back *out of obscurity* to push them into the light *for their own sake*" (VS1023, F783, emphasis added). These are the hidden actions "valued only by each man in himself" (VS1018–19, F779).

The only appeal of hiddenness that would be effective with the great, who value honor more than life itself, is the appeal to the noble, "the higher things." And this is exactly what Montaigne does: he rises *above* the highest, making it look easy. He rises above the highest point of the natural hierarchy of strength by taking the further step of renouncing the pride of despising death and being willing to appear weak and common. Montaigne displays this noble and free possibility to the great. He hides it—and he must hide it—in plain sight. His act is effective because he has gone first. The philosopher brings down the great with him, because philosophy has become a moral act. The "moralization of pride" is the elimination of the gentlemen.

The natural conflict between masters and slaves might be described as the conflict between the desire for mastery and recognition on the part of the strong and the desire for life itself on the part of the weak. The strong despise mere life in their desire for honor. The human self that is overcome or suppressed in the moralization of pride is the desire for mastery and recognition in the strong. Montaigne redirects natural spiritedness away from the visibility of the honorable to the hiddenness of the suppression of pride. In that respect, it could be said that he resolves the conflict in favor of the weak.

The effect Montaigne produces, then, is the overturning of the Aristotelian order. The high is now subjected to the low, the strong to the weak: "When I see both Caesar and Alexander, in the thick of their great tasks, so fully enjoying natural and therefore necessary and just pleasures, I do not say that that is relaxing their souls, I say that it is toughening them, subordinating these violent occupations and laborious thoughts, by the vigor of their spirits, to the practice of everyday life: wise men, had they believed that this [the violent] was their ordinary occupation, the other [the everyday] the extraordinary" (VS1108, F850). Caesar and Alexander are toughening, strengthening their souls in submitting to the practice of everyday life, disappearing into the ordinary. Montaigne rises above the highest of the traditional hierarchy by willingly submitting to the lowest. Life itself, "mere life" becomes good in itself, chosen for its own sake. "Life should be an aim unto itself, a purpose unto itself" (VS1051–52, F805).

The role of philosophy in the premodern world was to order that world by its place as the highest. Montaigne's internalization of strength is the act in which he judges and subjects the natural desire for recognition as the highest and strongest, the act through which he rises above the natural hierarchy of weak and strong. When he overcomes and renounces the pride of despising death, the effect that he produces is peace, through the resolution of the natural conflict between masters and slaves. The new philosophical act "frees the slaves" and "eliminates the gentlemen." By effacing himself and submitting to the lowest, Montaigne takes the momentous step that is necessary to reorder the world and bring into being a new order.

The Liberal Order

My discussion of the liberal order is intended to set out the framework within which civility becomes the social bond. The origin and justification of liberalism can be found in Machiavelli, Hobbes, Locke, Hume, Rousseau, and other modern political philosophers, each presenting his own account of the new political order. Montaigne does not offer a systematic account of liberalism, but he does present the outlines of this modern liberal order in which man is subject only to himself. If man is to be ordered to himself by himself, and if he is to be complete in himself, then he must be freed from the authority of nature and tradition and must submit only to an authority of his own making. Man ruling himself does not mean one man ruling another. It means setting up a nonhuman authority to which all can submit on equal terms.

Liberalism, as it appears in the *Essays*, is defined in terms of the rule of reason, the principles of representative government and the rule of law, and the freedom of the individual to pursue the good as he sees fit. The liberal order is the order of state and society that began to emerge in the early modern period of Western civilization.

Michael Oakeshott describes these changes that were taking place at the origins of modernity: "During the late fifteenth and sixteenth centuries, governments all over Europe were, in varying degrees, acquiring a power to control the activities and destinies of their subjects such as their predecessors had never enjoyed." Now "the tireless, inquisitive, roving hand of government was beginning to be able to reach everywhere, accustoming the subject to the notion that nothing should be beyond its grasp." According to Oakeshott, "the most significant of all these changes was . . . the gradual disappearance of the intermediate authorities which had formerly stood between a then weak central government and the subjects, leaving them naked before a power which in its magnitude was becoming comparable to a force of nature."[6]

Not coincidentally, the fourteenth and fifteenth centuries saw "the emergence . . . of the human individual in his modern idiom."[7] According to Oakeshott, the medieval condition of life was such that "relationships and allegiances normally sprang from status and rarely extricated themselves from the analogy of kinship. For the most part anonymity prevailed; individual human character was rarely observed because it was not there to be observed. What differentiated one man from another was insignificant when compared with what was enjoyed in common as members of a group of some sort."[8] The individual "became unmistakable when the habit appeared of engaging in activities identified as 'private': indeed, the appearance of 'privacy' in human conduct is the obverse of the desuetude of the communal arrangements from which modern individuality sprang."[9]

Oakeshott regards the emergence of this disposition to be an individual as "the pre-eminent event in modern European history."[10] Unsurprisingly, Montaigne is one of the exemplars of this disposition. "The disposition to regard a high degree of individuality in conduct and in belief as the condition proper to mankind and as the main ingredient of human 'happiness,' had become one of the significant dispositions of modern European character. What Petrarch did for one century, Montaigne did for another."[11]

In the *Essays*, Montaigne provides a philosophical foundation for the new liberal order of state and society. In "Of Custom" he writes: "Peoples brought up to liberty and to ruling themselves consider any other form of government monstrous and contrary to nature. Those who are accustomed to monarchy do the same. And whatever easy chance fortune offers them to change, even when with great difficulties they have rid themselves of the importunity of one master, they run to supplant him with a new one, with similar difficulties, because they cannot make up their minds to hate mastery itself" (VS116, F83–84). His claim, then, is that, whatever the regime may be, all traditional forms of rule are mastery because they are always the rule of men over each other. The inescapable rule of the strong over the weak is the powerful, unexamined hold of the tradition over the human mind. Men must learn to hate not this or that master but mastery itself. By reducing all forms of rule to mastery, Montaigne deliberately eliminates the traditional Aristotelian distinction between "political" rule and "despotic" rule, and the distinction between just and unjust regimes. He reduces all traditional forms of rule to tyranny, the most unjust regime, which is the rule of masters over slave.

If all traditional kinds of rule are forms of mastery, what is the new form of political life? If men learn to hate mastery, how will they tolerate rule at all? The new form of mastery cannot be the rule of men over each other. The new, unnatural form of rule is revealed in Montaigne's strange and surprising assertion: "A slave I must be only to reason" (VS794, F603). Strange and surprising since he hates mastery and slavery and seems to mistrust human reason. What must this reason be such that he can submit to it as a slave? It must be reason that he himself has originated, reason that is generated in the first moment of the philosophical act. Montaigne brings into being the new political form called the state: the state is a construct of reason.[12]

We can identify two kinds of reason presented in the *Essays*. The first is what might be called private or particular reason. Private reason is "an instrument of lead and of wax, stretchable, pliable, and adaptable to all biases and measures" (VS565, F425). Each man forges reason in himself. Therefore, reason has "many forms" (VS1065, F815). Private reason is the instrument of bias and self-interest.

The second kind of reason is not pliable but inflexible. Montaigne says: "There are few things on which we can give a sincere judgment, because there are few in which we have not in some way a private interest. Superiority and inferiority, mastery and subjection, are forced into a natural envy and contention; they must pillage one another perpetually. I do not believe either one about the rights of the other; let us leave it to reason, which is inflexible and impassive, when we are able to end it" (VS918, F701). Only reason inflexible and impassive can settle the conflict between masters and subjects, for reason inflexible is reason from which all bias and self-interest have been removed and is, therefore, the expression of the pure human will.

In "Of the Useful and the Honorable," we find a further specification of what reason inflexible and impassive means. Discussing the situation of the prince who is torn between doing what is honorable by keeping his word and betraying his honor by breaking his promises, Montaigne says that the prince who breaks his word in this urgent circumstance "has abandoned his own reason to a more universal and powerful reason" (VS799, F607). Reason inflexible is "universal" and "powerful" reason, which takes precedence over private reason and which has no conscience: it does what has to be done.

Reason, separated from human particularity, is the expression and instrument of the pure human will and exists as a philosophical invention. Since men must learn to hate mastery itself, the new form of rule must not appear to be mastery. "The state as a political form is not visible" and does not "appear." It is not visible to the eyes because "it does not exist outside of thought."[13] Further, it is essential that the philosophical origin of the new, unnatural rule be hidden because its origin must not be seen as the work of any human being. The prince must not have a human face. The new master must be "a faceless prince."[14] The power of the prince depends upon this hiddenness: "The people only adhere to this new order as long as they do not perceive the face of the new master."[15] Man submits to the master that he himself has made.

While the idea of the rule of reason may seem "abstract," in the new liberal order it takes the concrete form of representative government, the form of rule that Benjamin Constant calls a "discovery of the moderns."[16] The principle of ancient constitutions is the regime; the principle of modern constitutions is representation. Whereas a regime is rule embodied in those who rule, representation is the separation of rule from human beings.[17]

We see this modern notion of representation in Hobbes: "A person is he whose words or actions are considered, either as his own, or as representing the words or actions of an other man, or of any other thing to whom they are attributed, whether Truly or by Fiction. When they are considered as his owne, then he is called a Naturall Person: And when they are considered as representing the words and actions of an other, then he is a Feigned or Artificiall person." Rule, then, is representation of the will of every man: "A Multitude of men, are made One Person, when they are by one man, or one Person, Represented; so that it be done with the consent of every one of that Multitude in particular."[18] The only way that a multitude of men can erect such a common power "is to con-ferre all their power and strength upon one Man, or upon one Assembly of men, that may reduce all their Wills, by plurality of voices, unto one Will."[19] Reason inflexible and universal is the expression and instrument of the pure human will, the will without particularity. The true "prince," the new master, is this pure human will.

Montaigne served two terms as mayor of Bordeaux. Speaking of his own exercise of rule, he says that "the Mayor and Montaigne have always been two, with a very clear separation" (VS1012, F774). No man is essen-tially a prince or a prince by nature. Overcoming natural mastery requires separating the man from the prince so that the power of the prince is no longer in the service of the particular man.

We recognize the separation of the man from the prince, that rule is representation, and that the master is invisible when we speak about the peaceful transfer of power (the power does not belong by right to the individual who exercises it) and about respecting the office of the presi-dent (not necessarily the man who occupies it). We recognize that the man does not rule in his own name or by right and that, in principle, he merely does the will of the people as expressed in the laws made by their representatives in Congress.

On the one hand, the separation of the man from the prince in rep-resentative government is supposed to remove the private will and pas-sions of the natural man from the exercise of rule. The true prince is the channel of the pure human will, the will from which all particularity has been removed.[20] If rule is representation, then men cannot satisfy them-selves in ruling because they do not rule as natural men, only as repre-sentatives of the will of all. There is no place for honor or glory in simply doing the will of others. The principle of representation takes the honor out of rule.

On the other hand, the separation of the man from the prince means that the conscience of the man is not burdened with the betrayals of the prince. The rule of reason is not bound by the constraints of morality. When Montaigne describes the situation of the prince who is torn between the honorable action of keeping his word and the necessity of breaking his word, he is describing the situation of the man who happens to be the prince. The representative must not confuse his private conscience with the pure human will, of which he is merely the executor. The separation of the man from the prince is the separation of morality from politics and the privatization of the moral life.

The rule of law is the way in which the rule of reason expresses itself and asserts its authority, for the rule of law is distinguished from the rule of men and from the imposition of any man's private will. Montaigne says: "Necessity associates men and brings them together. This accidental link afterward takes the form of laws; for there have been some as savage as any human opinion can produce, which have nevertheless maintained their bodily health and long life as well as those of Plato and Aristotle could do" (VS956, F730). The only reason that men unite is that they depend on each other for the necessities of life. They do not naturally associate with each other for the pleasure of the association or for the pursuit of the good life. Montaigne calls necessity an "accidental link." The accidental link of necessity is replaced by the deliberate link of the agreement that is the promise to live under the laws. As he says, these laws can be savage; nevertheless they serve the purpose of keeping men together in peace.

Pierre Manent explains the meaning and purpose of law in modern political life. "For the reasons that are particularly highlighted by Montaigne's analysis of the human world, from a certain date Europeans abandoned every idea of a universal criterion of human actions, of a natural law or natural justice capable of guiding the legislator. With the exception of those who still subscribed to the Thomistic tradition, as it were all the authors who can hold our attention today abandoned, or rather, explicitly rejected, every idea of an objective human good, a good that could be discerned as such by human reason and on which, consequently, people could agree."[21] Therefore, "the just order, or the order of the only possible justice, is an order in which we ourselves establish the law as law, we ourselves posit the law as law."[22] We give this law to ourselves, because law is made by our representatives who express our own will. Laws, then, are concerned only with the conditions of acting, not with any substantive good to be attained in common. "While the ancient law directly guided and motivated action, the new law aims to produce the conditions of free movement."[23] Any substantive notion of the good would be the imposition of a private will. Therefore, as Oakeshott explains, laws are "the product of a pact or an agreement, not to act in concert but to acknowledge the authority of certain conditions in acting."[24]

Montaigne says: "Laws remain in credit not because they are just, but because they are laws. That is the mystic foundation of their authority; they have no other. And that is a good thing for them. They are often made by fools, more often by people who, in their hatred of equality, are wanting in equity; but always by men, vain and irresolute authors. There is nothing so grossly and widely and ordinarily faulty as the laws. Whoever obeys them because they are just, does not obey them for just the reason he should" (VS1072, F821). The authority of the laws rests not upon their claim to be just but on their "mystic" power as the expression of the pure human will, the will without particularity. The laws are made by men, yet the "mystic foundation" of the authority of the laws gives the rule of merely human law a kind of supernatural sanction.

Philosophy frees the slaves in the sense that one man will no longer be the master of another man. But the price of this freedom is the submission of all to the absolute power of the new monstrous and unnatural master. The condition of peace is the condition of equality, the elimination of the distinction between masters and slaves so that all are equal before the invisible philosopher-prince. This kind of equality, then, is not natural equality: it originates in the submission of all to the new master. "With respect to rule one might say that all men are created equal, but not by nature and not by God, but by their own invention. They invent their equality by inventing a superior that does not naturally exist."[25] There must be no pride in the new man, then, because all must submit to the prince, and no man can be permitted to rival the master's claim to rule. Thus, as Hobbes says, "in the presence of the master, the servants are equal, and without any honor at all; so are the subjects in the presence of the sovereign."[26]

Civil society is the counterpart of the state, for it is the arena of equality in which the individual is left free to pursue the good life as he sees fit. Montaigne rejects the standard of the common good and argues that, since philosophy has not been able to find a way to the good that is common, "let each one seek it in his particularity!" (VS622, F471). Society is the space of the freedom of the individual to find the satisfaction of his particularity. For Hegel, the first principle of civil society is "the concrete person who, as a *particular* person, as a totality of needs and a mixture of natural necessity and arbitrariness, is his own end."[27]

The features of a society that can be called "civil" follow from this description. First, civil society is the space of freedom that is permitted by the state, and therefore, it does not limit the power of the state. In the old order, philosophy had been a limit on political power, but an ineffective limit. For Montaigne, princely power is power "without measure" (VS917, F700), having no natural limit. "The state, or sovereign, is undetermined by anything except its own will and to anything except by its own will. This indetermination, the absence of any determination outside its own act, is the state's power or right."[28] The new form of mastery is absolute power that cannot be limited by anything above itself. To have anything above itself to limit it would be to make man again incomplete in himself.

Hobbes sets out both the meaning of society as this space of the freedom of the individual and the limits of that freedom. The liberty of the subject is found in those areas of life that the sovereign power has declined to regulate, such as the freedom to buy and sell, to enter contracts, to choose where he will live, how he will educate his children, how to make his living. Such liberties, at least in part, are set out in our Bill of Rights as limits placed on the power of the state over freedom of assembly, freedom of religion, freedom of the press, the right to bear arms, and so on. But Hobbes insists that these freedoms are not absolute.[29] It is always ultimately up to the master, the will of the people, to determine if and when these liberties are to be abridged or forfeited. The Constitution can be amended and amendments can be repealed.

Second, because it is the sphere of individual freedom, society is not the arena where men compete for the honor of ruling. Therefore, civil society is "society from which what is political has been removed."[30] The character that Montaigne displays in the essays is the character of a man who desires neither to rule nor be ruled, neither to command nor be commanded, and to live "outside of all subjection and mastery" except that of the laws (VS917, F700). Society is the depoliticized space where individuals must leave each other the freedom to pursue the good in their particularity.

Third, because it is the association of equals, civil society tends to suppress the "higher things" and bring out into the light the "lower things," which are the things that all men have in common. Society is the new space created by the emergence of the private sphere into the public. As Hannah Arendt explains, for the ancient and, in some ways, even for the medieval world, only two spheres of human association existed, the private realm of the household and the public realm of political life. Society emerges "from the shadowy interior of the household into the light of the public sphere."[31] The private realm of the household had been seen in premodern times as imperfect and incomplete, because the most significant human goods could be pursued only in the political realm. The invention of society entails nothing less than the relocation of the pursuit of the good to the social rather than the political sphere of life.

For the premodern world, the private realm is hidden because some of the actions of private life are considered shameful. The actions of private life are the actions that are merely necessary—that is, unfree or servile—for they are associated with mere life. Montaigne tells us, in the very first words of his preface to the reader, that his "end" in this work is "domestic and private" (VS3, F2). Society is the domestic and private brought out into the public, thus the replacement of the public by the private. And that is precisely the action of the *Essays*: Montaigne writes about himself, a merely private man with no great deeds to boast of, revealing in public the hidden, intimate details of his private life and thus overcoming the shame of the private.

Arendt describes the emergence of society largely in terms of economic considerations: whereas economics had been confined to household management—Aristotle treats economics in book 1 of the *Politics*, where he discusses the household as the unit of the city—in the modern world, it becomes a public matter. Montaigne wants to free the economic sphere of life from the constraints of the law. He criticizes the French legal system for its intrusion into every aspect of private life and praises the "ingenious opinion" of Isocrates, who advised the king "to make the trades and negotiations of his subjects free, gratuitous, and lucrative, and their disputes and quarrels onerous" (VS117–18, F85).

The sexual is one of the most private aspects of life that Montaigne discusses openly, in violation of the norms of custom. His open speaking about the sexual is intended to emphasize the point that all men share the same origins. It is in order "to make us all equal" that nature has made us this way (VS877, F668–69). In "On Some Verses of Virgil" he discusses the erotic in a way that he admits goes beyond the limits of propriety. His license in discussing the sexual is intended to effect a transformed sense of shame and of honor. By going against the instinctual shame associated with sex as the private and hidden, he is weakening the power of the shame associated with the private, overcoming one of the most deeply ingrained of all customs.

Montaigne uses ancient philosophy in order to go out in public "a bit more decently" (VS546, F409). He emerges into the public wearing the fig leaf of ancient philosophy, bringing the needs of the body out of the hiddenness and shamefulness of the private. In the liberal order, the lower things emerge into the light, and the higher, noble things are hidden because nothing must be able to challenge the power of the new master, the state.

Fourth, civil society is the association of equals, but it is not community. For Montaigne, the idea of the common good is simply the "pretext of reason" for the actions of vicious men (VS802, F609–10). The idea of the common good is the deception perpetrated by particular, pliable, self-interested reason, which allows the strong to dominate the weak. Montaigne is a slave to reason, yet he surpasses "all modern examples" in his independence from others. He tries to have "no express need of anyone" (VS968, F739–40). This condition of being a slave to reason while, at the same time, being independent of all other men is explained in Hobbes's response to Cardinal Bellarmine's defense of the classical-Christian standard of the common good. Bellarmine's error is that he claims that "the Members of every Commonwealth, as of a naturall Body, depend one of another." Hobbes replies: "It is true, they cohaere together; but they depend onely on the Soveraign, which is the Soul of the Common-wealth;

which failing, the Commonwealth is dissolved into a Civill war, no one man so much as cohaering to another, for want of a common Dependance on a known Soveraign."[32] Rousseau, in his discussion of the social contract, sets out the same condition: the contract "guarantees [each citizen] against all personal dependence,"[33] so that "each citizen is in a position of perfect independence from all the others and of excessive dependence upon the City."[34]

Finally, civil society is not *moral* community: it is the space invented by philosophy for the freedom of particular human beings, not a condition of mutual moral dependence. "It is the web of associations formed by the interactions of individuals as they seek the fulfillment of the purposes peculiar to them as individuals pursuing their private happiness."[35] In Montaigne's words, "Let each one seek the good in his particularity." The individual has no need of anyone for the good, but only for the necessities of life, for biological, economic necessity. Anything "higher" than that is his own private concern. The good is no longer a matter of public agreement but a private choice.

How, then, can these free individuals live together in peace without a common good to unite them? The moral virtues of the tradition, which have their place in a moral community, cannot be the bond that holds men together in such a society. In the new liberal order, authenticity and inauthenticity are the possibilities for moral life, and the new social bond of civility replaces the tradition.

THREE

Authenticity

The Greatest Thing in the World

The difference between the moral community formed by tradition and the bond that unites individuals in modern civil society can be seen in the contrast between Aristotle's admonition "One ought not even consider that a particular citizen belongs to himself, but rather that all belong to the city; for each is a part of the city"[1] and Montaigne's assertion that "the greatest thing in the world is to know how to belong to oneself" (VS242, F178). Belonging to oneself is the moral condition that we refer to today as "authenticity." Civility is the way in which individuals who belong to themselves conduct themselves toward each other in civil society.

The Essays of Michel de Montaigne embody, even in their title, the way of being human that, almost four centuries after their publication, came to be called "authenticity." Montaigne never uses the term "authenticity" to describe his own way of being: that term was not in use in French in the sixteenth century. However, when he says that "the greatest thing in the world is to know how to belong to oneself," he captures the philosophical meaning of authenticity and shows how authenticity became possible in the turn to modern philosophy.

The ordinary, prephilosophical meaning of "authenticity" in its primary sense refers to the origin of the thing in question, the certitude attached to the origin or author of a work of some kind. A document or artifact is authentic if it actually comes from the origin it purports to be from. The text or work is "original," not a copy or forgery. So, for example, an authentic Vermeer is a painting that actually came from the hand of Vermeer and is, therefore, an "original" Vermeer.

The *Oxford English Dictionary* gives the philosophical meaning of authenticity as "a mode of existence arising from self-awareness, critical reflection on one's goals and values, and responsibility for one's own actions." Authenticity is "the condition of being true to oneself." This formulation of the philosophical meaning is said to be derived from Heidegger's *Being and Time*: "Mineness belongs to any existent Dasein, and belongs to it as the condition which makes authenticity and inauthenticity possible."[2]

Francis Slade explains how it happens that authenticity replaces traditional ethics: "In what can be considered to be the fundamental sentence of *Sein und Zeit* Heidegger asserts that 'possibility stands higher than actuality,' which means that there are no ends, there are only purposes, or as Heidegger calls them, 'projects' (*Entwurf*). This is why ethics disappears from the account of human existence in *Sein und Zeit* to be replaced by authenticity (*Eigentlichkeit*) and resoluteness (*Entschlossenheit*)."[3]

In this chapter, I set out the meaning of authenticity as it appears in Montaigne's *Essays*. Authenticity—knowing how to belong to oneself—is grounded in the primacy of possibility and the replacement of naturally given ends by "projects." Montaigne makes himself to be what he wants to be: he is his own project.

A FORM ALL ONE'S OWN

In the classical-Christian tradition, the human being is complete only in relation to the divine and the eternal. The meaning of human completeness is understood as inherent in the very nature of man, the nature that he does not choose but that is given to him. In the Aristotelian account, human nature is explained in terms of the metaphysical categories of "form" and "end." Form is "what" a thing is, and what a thing is depends entirely on the species to which it belongs, the *kind* of thing it is. Form is the set of characteristics that is essential to a being of its kind and is, therefore, universal, belonging to all of the members of a species and accounting for why they are the way they are. Individuals are "particulars," and particulars are always understood in relation to the universal: the form is the "common measure" by which every particular must be explained and judged. The human being is complete when he becomes what he ought to be, when he attains the end proper to him as a human being.

Ends are not human purposes but are given by nature: they are not chosen or intended by the being in question. We can choose to act or not act in accordance with our given end, but we do not choose the end itself. In other words, we are not free to choose what will complete and satisfy us. That satisfaction is *determined* by our very nature as human beings. The difference between ends and purposes is that "ends exist independently of our willing them to be; they do not originate in our willing them to be. Purposes take their origin from our willing them; purposes would not be if agents did not give them being. . . . [For Aristotle] happiness is the end of human life whatever the purposes of human beings may be. Happiness is the end not because I choose happiness and make it my purpose, but because of what I am, the intrinsic character, or nature, of the human being itself."[4]

The natural completion, perfection, fulfillment, and, therefore, the satisfaction of the being is its end: it becomes what it *should be* as a perfect member of its species through the actualization of the potentialities that belong to the species. Becoming is always actualization of what was already there potentially: becoming or actualization takes place only through the agency of final cause. What is possible for the individual is determined by its nature as a member of the species.

Ethics is concerned with the human good, the end that is proper to the human being. The end is the good that is the same for all members of a given species. Therefore, the attainment of the natural end is the satisfaction of the particular: the particular is satisfied in the possession of the good that belongs to him by nature. Both moral virtue and contemplation constitute the perfection, completion, and satisfaction of the human being. Both moral virtue and the philosophical life are dependent upon community: the morally virtuous man for the practice of virtue and the philosopher for the condition of leisure. The political community exists for the sake of the common good, and philosophy is essential to the common good.

Montaigne's emancipation of man from nature, his act of reordering man to man, entails a radical change in the meaning of human completeness. Authenticity is the completeness of the new man, because it is the completion of the modern philosophical act, the two moments of detachment and reordering. The philosopher's link with all men is that he needs a body, but in his case, it is a reappropriation of the body from which he has first been separated. To be within the world is to be embodied. Self-possession is the act in which the philosopher, separated from the natural man, reappropriates the natural man in his concrete particularity and becomes whole as a new man. Therefore, authenticity is not a natural but a philosophical condition, for it has a philosophical origin.

The man who is astonished at himself as the new figure of the philosopher is the man who has been transformed by the philosophical act, the man in whom the philosophical act has become self-conscious. His new character is the way he lives as the philosopher united with the natural man and the way he lives among other men. The authentic individual is complete in himself: he needs no one and depends on no one for what he is as a moral and intellectual being. In particular, he needs no recognition or honor from those among whom he lives.

The rejection of naturally given ends, replacing them with human purposes, makes possible a new kind of freedom that Hegel describes as the principle of the modern world. "The right of the subject's *particularity* to find satisfaction, or—to put it differently—the right of *subjective freedom*, is the pivotal and focal point in the difference between *antiquity* and the *modern* age. This right, in its infinity, is expressed in Christianity, and it has become the universal and actual principle of a new form of the world."[5]

Freedom in the modern world—the "new form of the world"—is freedom from naturally given ends-in-themselves and therefore freedom from nature. The metaphysics of form and final cause, of potentiality and actuality, does not allow for the coming into being of the genuinely new, because becoming is always simply actualization of potentialities given by nature and belonging to the species. The genuinely new can emerge only as the possible. Potentialities and actualities are given by nature; possibilities are invented and made real by the mind freed from the constraints of nature. That is why the elevation of possibility over actuality means that freely chosen projects replace naturally given ends in human life. That is how the satisfaction of the particular in his freedom becomes the principle of the new form of the world.

"The new form of the world" is the world brought into being by Montaigne. Montaigne uses the language of form and end, but he replaces ends with projects and elevates the possible over the actual. Becoming, without a naturally given end, becomes not the actualization of potentiality but the bringing into being of the possible. This new becoming is the metaphysical condition for the self-possession that is authenticity. Modern man, the incommensurable particular, finds his satisfaction in his own freely chosen projects, not in the attainment of naturally given ends. For the authentic particular, his project is himself: to be, to make himself, what he wants to be.

Authentic self-possession must be distinguished from what might be described as natural self-possession, the natural experience of one's particularity. There are two modes of this natural self-possession. Naïve, natural self-possession is the mode of belonging to oneself "without striving" that Montaigne finds in the uneducated, simple, and ignorant. This is an unselfconscious condition of being one with oneself that is characterized by ease and absence of conflict within oneself. The self-possession of one who strives for excellence, on the other hand, is the experience of the anticipated perfection and completion of himself as a human being. This completion is achieved through struggle, by conforming himself to the model of perfect virtue, whether intellectual or moral, forming himself by the inherited, learned standard of the tradition. Both kinds of self-possession remain within nature, and both are presumptuous, the former in a naïve, unreflective way and the latter on account of the submission to the inherited tradition.

Montaigne's authentic self-possession is different from both kinds of natural self-possession. Unlike the naïve self-possession of the simple, his self-possession is self-conscious. Unlike those who strive for the self-possession that comes with conformity to the standard of excellence, Montaigne does not want to be what he should be—that is, what he would be if he attained the perfection of the human form. He wants to be what he makes himself to be, what he can be, freed from the constraints of nature. That means giving up the old order, rejecting the standard of form and final cause, and giving up his natural particularity with its natural satisfaction. There is, then, a fundamental difference between natural self-possession and the new self-possession that is the condition for authenticity. Montaigne's authentic self-possession is the reorigination of his form, making it his own and reordering himself to himself.

As I have argued in chapter 1, the first step in freeing himself from nature is the renunciation of the status and self-esteem to which he is entitled in the old order. His judgment has been purified of the presumption of natural self-possession, making his judgment his own in a new way. Judgment is not the receptive act of those who simply accept the tradition from the ancients. Montaigne's judgment "trans-forms" the given and inherited. Judgment is a "work" that is "all his own."

Natural judgment is the act of the mind in which the particular is subsumed under the universal: the particular is judged according to whether or not, or to what extent, he has attained the perfection of the natural form. Montaigne's judgment is different from natural judgment: there is no universal form by which every human being can be measured. Instead, each man naïvely presumes that he himself is the universal. "It seems to each man that the ruling pattern of nature is in him; to this he refers all other forms as to a touchstone. The ways that do not square with his are counterfeit and artificial. What brutish stupidity!" (VS725, F548). The traditional philosopher above all is guilty of this presumption, because he sees himself as the most complete and perfect form of human being. Purified of the self-esteem of the philosopher, Montaigne does not presume that he is the universal.

Montaigne's nonpresumptuous judgment regards himself and others as incommensurable particulars, incommensurable because there is no common measure. In "Of Repentance" Montaigne says: "There is no one who, if he listens to himself, does not discover in himself *a form all his own*, a master form" (VS811, F615, emphasis added). The idea of a form that is "all his own" is the complete reversal of the traditional idea of form.

A form that is all one's own is the self-possession that is authenticity. Authentic self-possession means the particularization of form.

"Of Cato the Younger" begins with a statement of Montaigne's practice of judgment as it relates to the particularization of form. He does not share the common error of judging another by the standard of himself, and he easily believes that another man may have qualities different from his. "Because I feel myself tied down to one form, I do not oblige everybody to espouse it, as all others do. I believe in and conceive a thousand contrary ways of life, and in contrast with the common run of men, I more easily admit difference than resemblance between us. I am as ready as you please to acquit another man from sharing my conditions and principles. I consider him simply in himself, without relation to others; I mold him to his own model. . . . I have a singular desire that we should each be judged in ourselves apart, and that I may not be measured in conformity with the common examples" (VS229, F169). Montaigne has freed himself from the common error of presumption. He judges each man as he is in himself, not by the common measure of form and final cause.

The description of himself that best captures Montaigne's self-originated form, his incommensurable particularity, is "the self-ordered soul." Montaigne asks himself: "And then, for whom do you write?" The learned, who pass judgment on books, recognize only erudition and art and value only learning. Common and popular souls, on the other hand, cannot recognize the grace and the weight of lofty and elevated discourse. These two human types almost exhaust the possibilities; nevertheless, there is a third possibility. "The third type into whose hands you fall, that of souls ordered and strong in themselves, is so rare that for this very reason it has neither name nor rank among us: it is time half lost to aspire and strive to please them" (VS657, F498). The capacity to order oneself is freedom of judgment: "Indeed there are few souls so regulated, so strong and well-born, that they can be trusted to their own conduct, and who are able, with moderation and without temerity, to sail in the liberty of their judgments beyond the common opinions" (VS559, F419–20). "Ordering" implies an end, a direction to some goal. The term "self-ordered" means that he is not directed by nature to a given end, but directs himself to his own freely chosen purposes. The self-ordered soul has no name or rank: it cannot be explained or contained within the natural hierarchy. Because the self-ordered soul has no name or rank, it is a hidden, unrecognized new type, a new possibility of human being brought into being by Montaigne himself.

In his description of the modern freedom of the particular, Hegel writes: "It is only by raising what is present and given to a self-creating process that the higher sphere of the good is attained."[6] The self-ordered soul reoriginates his own form by reordering what is given and present. He is his own project, making himself to be what he wants to be. As Montaigne says: "I employ myself entirely upon myself" (VS1003, F766), and, "I have put all my efforts into forming my life" (VS784, F596).

How is what is present and given raised to a self-creating process? The philosophical mind confronts the world as a world of accidents. Nature has to be seen not in terms of forms and ends but in terms of mere accidents, material to be formed and directed by the mind. In the sphere of ethics, the materials to be formed and ordered are the passions, inclinations, instincts, and impressions of the natural man.

Throughout the essays, Montaigne returns to the beginnings, the origins, of what he is, of why he is the way he is. These beginnings and origins seem to be accidental. He treats even "nature" as an accidental origin, not a permanent given. He is just a collection of accidents, not an instance of a universal form. He just happened to be born with a certain temperament, and he has become what he is by accident. In "Of Cruelty" he writes: "My virtue is a virtue, or I should say an innocence, that is accidental and fortuitous. If I had been born with a more unruly disposition, I fear it would have gone pitifully with me. For I have not experienced much firmness in my soul to withstand passions, if they are even the least bit vehement. I do not know how to foster quarrels and conflict within me. Thus I cannot give myself any great thanks because I find myself free from many vices" (VS427, F311). He does not know whether his goodness was "infused" into him from his father, or whether the good examples and education of his childhood "insensibly" contributed to his nature, or whether "for some other reason" he was born with a good disposition (VS427, F311). But whatever the reason, he was just born that way. "What good I have in me I have . . . by the chance of my birth. I have gotten it neither from law, nor from precept nor from any other apprenticeship" (VS429, F313). This account of his goodness looks like naïve, natural self-possession: it hides the true becoming of what he is. Authenticity, the greatest thing in the world, must look like naïve, natural self-possession, because greatness must be hidden.

Forming the Civil Disposition

Montaigne subjects his natural, accidental characteristics to his judgment. Judgment allows him to see the truth about himself, because his judgment is without self-esteem. Through judgment he re-forms himself, sometimes affirming and sometimes rejecting what he is by accident. Judgment, then, is the act of evaluating, ranking, and ordering. Montaigne's "reform" of himself is far more radical than the reform achieved through the deliberate pursuit of moral excellence. The man of perfect virtue rules his passions and inclinations, directing and moderating them by reason to conform to the standard of perfection. Montaigne, however, goes back to the very beginnings of his inclinations and passions, changing his natural disposition.

The meaning of traditional virtue is strength, and this strength is the basis for mastery over oneself and others: "The Romans took the general term 'virtue' from their word for 'strength'. . . . It is probable that the first virtue that manifested itself among men and gave some advantage over others was this one, by which the strongest and most courageous made themselves masters of the weaker and acquired particular rank and reputation; whence it has retained this linguistic honor and dignity. Or else that these nations, being very warlike, gave the prize and the worthiest title to the one virtue which was most familiar to them" (VS384, F277).

For Montaigne, virtue is no longer a matter of superior strength. In "Of the Education of Children" he directs himself to the upbringing of the nobleman. What he has to offer in the way of advice concerning this most difficult topic is "this new lesson," the "ease" of virtue (VS162, F120). The young man's tutor "will teach him this new lesson, that the value and the height of true virtue lies in the ease, utility, and pleasure of its practice, which is so far from being difficult that children can master it as well as men, the simple as well as the subtle. Virtue's tool is moderation [*le reglement*], not strength. Socrates, her prime favorite, *deliberately gives up his strength*, to slip into the naturalness and ease of her gait" (VS162, F120, emphasis added). Self-regulation, then, is not the same as self-mastery. Socrates deliberately gives up his strength, so that his virtue is like the virtue of the simple. Virtue looks "natural," with no effort or struggle. The self-ordered soul is *strong in itself*. But the self-directing man does not appear as strong or morally superior. Rather he appears as weak, because there is no struggle or difficulty in his actions. The highest form of authenticity is to appear unselfconsciously natural.

Montaigne gives us two descriptions of the practice of his easy virtue: "unlearning evil" and "training the disposition." In "Of Cruelty" he explains his own natural goodness in terms of Antisthenes' understanding of the best apprenticeship for virtue: "to unlearn evil" (VS428, F311). Throughout the *Essays*, Montaigne presents his own weak way of coming to terms with the accidents of life and with the occasions that force us to confront evil. In "Of Husbanding Your Will" he explains that his way involves avoiding such occasions whenever possible. Some philosophers have taken another way: they have not feared to seek out trials and test their powers of endurance in wrestling with misfortunes. But, Montaigne says, "Let us not tackle these examples; we would not come up to them. . . . For our common souls there is too much effort and harshness in that. . . . We little men must flee the storm from farther away; we must try to avoid feeling it, not try to endure it" (VS1015, F777). Later in the same essay, he writes: "Passions are as easy for me to avoid as they are hard for me to moderate. . . . He who cannot attain that noble impassibility of the Stoics, let him take refuge in the bosom of this plebeian stupidity of mine. What those men did by virtue, I train myself to do by disposition" (VS1019–20, F780).

How does Montaigne propose to deal with the passions? Passions, he says, are easy for him to avoid. Since the beginnings of all things are weak, he confronts the passions in their weak beginnings rather than test himself against them when they have reached their height. "If each man watched closely the effects and circumstances of the passions that dominate him, as I have done with the ones I have fallen prey to, he would see them coming and would check their impetuosity and course a bit. They do not always leap at our throats at a single bound; there are threats and degrees" (VS1074, F822–23). Stopping the passion in its beginnings makes it possible to avoid the struggle between reason and passion.[7]

In his essay on anger, Montaigne provides a concrete and detailed example of the way he deals with that passion. Since we incorporate anger into ourselves by hiding it so that it grows and festers inside ourselves, he does not try to hide his anger. The passions, he says, grow weak when we vent and express them. "When I get angry, it is as keenly, but also as briefly and privately, as I can" (VS719, F544). He loses his temper but he does not hurl insults at everyone around him. "Easily I keep from getting into this passion, and I am strong enough, if I am expecting it, to repel its onslaught, however violent its cause; but if it once occupies and seizes me, it carries me away, however inane its cause" (VS720, F544). Montaigne concludes this essay with a reflection on Aristotle that reveals something of the difference between them. Aristotle claims that anger sometimes serves as a weapon for valor and for virtue. Montaigne, however, is focused on the power that this passion has over us: "We move other weapons, this one moves us; our hand does not guide it, it guides our hand; it holds us, we do not hold it" (VS720, F545). The Aristotelian teaching concerning the mastery and direction of the passions is ineffective.

Montaigne does feel the passions. However, his attitude toward them is not a matter of mastering them by the force of reason but of choosing the passions that he allows himself to feel and those that he wants to avoid. For Aristotle, the passions themselves are neither good nor evil: what matters is the rule of reason over the passions. But for Montaigne, certain passions are vicious in themselves.

The way in which Montaigne understands and deals with the passions is also illustrated in "Of Diversion," where he tells how he led a young prince away from the passion of vengeance: "I let the passion alone" (VS835, F634). He does not try to persuade the prince to directly confront the passion of vengeance. Rather, Montaigne diverts him to ambition because ambition is a lesser vice than vengeance. Thus, the role of the passions is different for Montaigne than it is for Aristotle: Montaigne uses one passion to counter another, more harmful one.[8] He avoids the struggle between reason and passion, thereby minimizing the role of mastery in the practice of virtue. Further, he diverts the prince by means of an image of the honor and goodwill to be gained by mercy and kindness, thus affecting the prince's judgment of the true meaning of honor and leading him away from the customary view that honor is primarily a matter of avenging insults.

Most of Montaigne's examples of passions to be avoided have to do with the violent passions associated with revenge (such as anger and pride), and his examples of the passions to be encouraged are those having to do with compassion and forgiveness (such as pity). Giving up self-esteem, deliberately giving up one's strength, and avoiding the violent passions associated with vengeance all show that the traditional meaning of honor is being revalued.

Although "training the disposition" sounds much like the habituation to virtue described by Aristotle, Montaigne is here in fact distinguishing between the two: his reform deliberately adopts a disposition of "plebian stupidity" rather than struggling to master his passions in the manner of the strong. The disposition is the temperament one is born with; it is given by nature. "Unlearning evil" and "training the disposition" both show that naturalness can be deliberately acquired.

Montaigne shows that he is indeed attempting a radical reform of the moral life and that the reform he wants to effect occurs at the deepest level of action; it is a reform of the beginnings, the springs of action. "Those who in my time have tried to correct the world's *mores* by new opinions, reform the superficial vices; the essential ones they leave as they were." These "external, arbitrary reforms" cost little and bring public acclaim, leaving "the other natural, consubstantial, and internal vices" unaffected (VS811, F615). He criticizes those who concern themselves with the correction of trivial faults and "the vices of appearance" rather than the vices of reality. "Oh what an easy and applauded route those superficial men take, compared with ours!" (VS888, F677). Montaigne is not attempting to reform through new opinions. Rather he is attempting to reform judgment itself, a reform so difficult and so deep because it is the reformation of nature itself. He *makes* his new disposition natural: he reoriginates his disposition.

This reorigination of himself reveals the way in which ethics has become philosophical, how it is grounded in the modern philosophical act. He has given up his old, natural particularity and re-formed himself as a new nature. This is not the old notion of ruling the passions, nor is it a merely superficial change of opinions. Rather it is the complete revaluing of good and evil in accordance with his reordering of man to man.

REFLECTION AND DOUBLENESS

How is it possible to become the origin of oneself? Becoming the origin of what you are looks impossible: it seems that you would have to exist before you exist. How can you create the condition for the possibility of bringing yourself into being?

The condition for the possibility of authentic self-possession is doubleness. Doubleness is inherent in Montaigne's very first step of renouncing self-esteem and overcoming natural presumption, for this makes it possible for him to detach himself from himself and see himself as he is. That is the stance of *reflection* that he assumes in order to write his essays. The detached observer sees his body and interacts with his body in a way that is different from the interaction of body and soul in the natural man.

Montaigne changes his "nature." Yet he presents himself as if he were just born this way. The self-ordered soul is "well born." He uses the term for the natural event of being "born" for the nonnatural philosophical act of self-origination. He does this because he hides his own self-origination. Authenticity looks like this kind of transparency and ease, in which there is no conflict or struggle. It has to look like naïve, natural self-possession, without the "striving" of final cause. That is why he compares himself to shop apprentices and workmen, to his gardener and his muleteer. He takes no credit for his goodness. Therefore, he has no self-esteem. He has given up the pride and self-esteem of the few who have attained the perfection of the old order. He takes no credit because he has forgotten his old particularity.

Montaigne's self-origination is the doubleness of "the left hand not knowing what the right hand is doing." That is why he talks as if he were just born this way. The doubleness that forgets itself allows him to possess himself without self-esteem. This self-forgetful self-possession is the completeness of authenticity, and this completeness is his satisfaction.

Montaigne says that there is no struggle within himself, yet being true to oneself requires a kind of doubling of oneself in order to judge oneself and to be one with what you have brought into being. In this way, he becomes his own judge. Judgment is conscience. "Those of us especially who live a private life that is on display only to ourselves must have a pattern established within us by which to test our actions, and, according to this pattern, now pat ourselves on the back, now punish ourselves. I have my own laws and court to judge me, and I address myself to them more than anywhere else. . . . Others do not see you . . . . Therefore do not cling to their judgment; cling to your own" (VS807, F613). He judges himself by the standard of himself, his own self-originated form, not by the natural standard of perfection.

Thus, authenticity has replaced traditional ethics. The natural standard of perfection is the completion of the human form in activities that are ends in themselves. From that standpoint, Montaigne looks imperfect and incomplete. In "Of Repentance" he writes: "Others form man; I tell of him, and represent a particular, very ill-formed" (VS804, F610 emended). In "To the Reader" he tells us from the outset that he will show himself as he is, without striving and with all his defects (VS3, F2). That is, he will appear without the perfection of the human form.

Here we see the shift in his judgment from the standard of natural perfection to the standard of what is his own. The *Essays* do not conceal his imperfections any more than does his portrait, which displays not a perfect face but his own face (VS148, F108). The *Essays* end with his new judgment of human perfection: it is an absolute perfection to know how to enjoy *our own* being rightly. Perfection is the enjoyment of "our own" being, our own *human* being, not participation in the divine condition. But we must "know how" to enjoy our own being "rightly." We must know how to make our being our own by a free act of judgment.

What looks like a lowering of moral standards is actually the rejection of the traditional hierarchy. Authenticity means just being what you *are*, not what you *should be*. But what you are is not just what you are accidentally and by nature. It means what you are when you have removed presumption and self-esteem and become the origin of yourself. And that is not natural. What looks like a lowering of standards and the rejection of heroic virtue—Cato tearing out his own entrails for the beauty of the thing itself—is really Montaigne's self-overcoming, the denial of his natural self. Cato shows us how far nature can go (VS231, F171). Montaigne, however, shows us a new kind of freedom, freedom from nature, achieved by man himself. The more his old, naturally given particularity is given up, the more he is "his own" by his free choice.

It is important to emphasize that Montaigne's authenticity is not about simply following his passions and inclinations. In *Montaigne and the Life of Freedom*, Felicity Green challenges the claim that Montaigne's goal in the *Essays* is the achievement of authenticity and argues that his goal is rather the attainment of freedom. On Green's interpretation, Montaigne's central goal is securing a sphere of liberty or freedom that he can properly call *his own*. She interprets the passages about "knowing how to belong to oneself" to refer to an idea of liberty rather than authenticity. Green supports her argument by showing how Montaigne reformulates ancient Stoic practices of self-regulation and self-awareness and how he rehabilitates these practices in order to establish a sphere of inner refuge and tranquility. This inner sphere is "free" in the sense of being free from the compulsion of the passions and free from the subjection to external authority.

My understanding of Montaigne's authenticity is not at odds with Green's account of his autonomy. "To have a sense of self . . . is to constitute oneself, not as an individual, but as an agent: autonomy, rather than identity, defines the limits of our innermost, essential self. To return to oneself, to belong to oneself, is to live within the scope of one's power and thereby free oneself both from the inward compulsion of the passions and from subjection to external objects, forces, and persons." Green, then, understands the self as a moral rather than a psychological or ontological category. "It names that sphere in which we may be said to act, instead of being acted upon: it is that which remains when all the accidental, contingent qualities conferred upon us by fortune are taken away, that dimension of our lives over which we are able to exercise a degree of power, and in respect of which we may be said to be free."[9]

In "Freedom and Self-Possession: The Case of Montaigne's *Essais*," she further explains that "the image that the text contains . . . is offered not as the intimate trace of an elusive, authentic self, but as the bold imprint and index of Montaigne's moral preoccupations and sensibility—a register of that which he can truly count his own. His book, in other words, represents him as he truly is—but as a witness of his moral character as a free man, not as an expression (sincere or otherwise) of his innermost psychological being."[10]

Green makes a compelling case that Montaigne's goal is freedom, and she brings out very clearly that his portrayal of the self is moral rather than psychological. However, she argues against the view that authenticity is Montaigne's goal, because she sees authenticity as opposed to freedom and identifies authenticity as "the subjective, private, solitary realm of inner impulses and dispositions." Authenticity, then, is subjection to the compulsion of the passions: "To cleave to oneself, to preserve oneself, is to be true to oneself, to live and write in a manner that reflects one's deepest, most spontaneous and particular intentions, inclinations and affinities." This version of authenticity is incompatible with freedom.[11]

Although authenticity may be characterized as Green presents it, my understanding of Montaigne's authenticity shows it to be compatible with the goal of freedom: authenticity is in fact a kind of freedom, the self-directing kind of freedom. Montaigne's authenticity is not subjection to the compulsion of the passions but a new way to deal with the passions that are mere "nature," to master "the accidental and contingent conferred on us by fortune." It is the freedom of choosing which of the passions to allow and which to put aside in the deliberate, free construction of the new moral character through which he becomes what he wants to be. Authenticity, as Montaigne presents it, requires an act of the will in its freedom to determine *itself*, to choose its end and direct the given to that end.

Montaigne orders his actions not to the naturally given end of perfection and completeness but to himself. He is the beginning and the end of his actions. "The range of our desires should be circumscribed and restrained to a narrow limit of the nearest and most contiguous good things; and moreover their course should be directed not in a straight line that ends up elsewhere, but in a circle whose two extremities by a short sweep meet and terminate in ourselves. Actions that are performed without this reflexive movement, I mean a searching and genuine reflexive movement—the actions, for example, of the avaricious, the ambitious, and so many others who run in a straight line, whose course carries them ever forward—are erroneous and diseased" (VS1011, F773). This "searching and genuine reflexive movement" (*reflexion voisine et essentielle*) is the return to himself that is necessary for authentic self-possession.

The authentic way of belonging to oneself and being true to oneself is to give up one's old particularity and to be the origin of what you are as the new particular. The *Essays* begin in Montaigne's desire to reveal himself and end in the satisfaction of that desire. The satisfaction of that desire, his self-revelation, is the achievement of perfect authenticity. The revelation of himself as weak and imperfect is the revelation of what looks like naïve natural self-possession. He "returns" to what looks like the "original" self-possession of every man, but this is really a new self-possession that includes within itself the renunciation of natural self-possession and the elevation of the present and given to the higher sphere of the good—that is, to self-creation. Perfect authenticity must be the hidden satisfaction of the philosopher, the left hand not knowing what the right hand is doing. As Montaigne says, the self-ordered soul has neither name nor rank among us. He is, therefore, invisible. The authentic individual must be content within himself, without the honor and recognition of his achievement. Honor is completely internalized: he is content with himself and his own judgment of himself.

Although there may seem to be a contradiction in saying both that he makes himself to be what he wants to be and that he is astonished at what he has become as if he himself had not done this, it is, in fact, not a contradiction. Montaigne, as he presents himself in the *Essays*, is the mind of the detached observer reunited with the natural man. The mind of the detached observer is working on the natural man, and because the detached observer is without self-esteem, he forms the natural man in a certain way—that is, without self-esteem. He forms him for private life. To have the mind of the detached observer is to be always open to the possible, which cannot be predicted. That is why he is astonished. He does make himself to be what he wants to be, but he does not know precisely what that will be until he comes upon himself, catches himself unawares, as a possibility brought forth by his thought in the act of essaying himself.

Perfect authenticity is the most complete renunciation of natural particularity and the bringing into being of the new, incommensurable particular. But how can this task ever be "complete"? Montaigne's satisfaction is not found in union with the divine and eternal through contemplation but in the temporal world. Since Montaigne's satisfaction is in "bringing into being"—that is, in becoming—his satisfaction is without "end." Montaigne says: "I do not portray being: I portray passing" (VS805, F611). Our being is in action and movement (VS386–87, F279), not in rest and permanence. Our being is in becoming. Becoming, for the authentic man, is the "creative process" of transforming what is "present and given," and what is present and given is always changing. The essays are the "tests," the experiments, for determining and bringing into being what is possible.

If satisfaction is experienced in completeness, how is it possible to have completeness and satisfaction without an end? Montaigne says, "My professed principle . . . is to be wholly contained and established within myself" (VS814–15, F618). Isn't self-containment a kind of completeness, a state of being "finished"? Because we are mortal, our satisfaction can only be in time. We can possess our own being only in time: "Without [time] nothing can be possessed" (VS1011, F773). Our satisfaction can only be temporal, temporary, because there is no ultimate, final end to which all of our actions are ordered. "The end is found of itself at the conclusion of every task" (VS1010, F773). As Hegel puts it: "What the subject *is*, *is the series of its actions*."[12]

Temporal satisfaction is a satisfaction that belongs to the imperfect and unfinished. The essays themselves capture this temporality, for they are, in this sense, without an end. "Who does not see that I have taken a road along which I shall go, without stopping and without effort, as long as there is ink and paper in the world?" (VS945, F721).

This contentment with becoming and with temporal satisfaction explains Montaigne's famous nonchalance. To be nonchalant about death, the final act, is to thoroughly embrace one's temporality and to be contained within oneself, directing all of one's actions, even the final act, to oneself. "I want a man to act, and to prolong the functions of life as long as he can; and I want death to find me planting my cabbages, but careless [*nonchalant*] of death, and still more of my unfinished [*imparfait*] garden" (VS89, F62). This allusion to his unfinished and imperfect garden calls to mind the perfect garden of Eden and Saint Augustine's experience of human life as exile from that garden: "Assuredly, Lord, I toil with this, toil within myself: I have become to myself a soil laborious and of heavy sweat. For I am not now considering the parts of the heavens or measuring the distances of the stars, or seeking how the earth is held in space; it is I who remember, I, my mind. It is not remarkable if things that I am not are far from my knowledge: but what could be closer to me than myself?"[13] Augustine is himself the laborious soil on which he works, yet he believes that he will not be complete until his toil is ended and he is united with his creator in the eternal rest and leisure of the Sabbath. For Montaigne, on the other hand, the *Essays* are his satisfaction in this world.

Montaigne turns philosophy into work. The mind's "principal and most laborious study is studying itself" (VS819, F621). He cannot stomach the contemplative ecstasies of Socrates, but he admires the Socrates "who brought human wisdom back down from heaven, where she was wasting her time, and restored her to man, with whom lies her most proper and laborious and useful business" (VS1038, F793). Philosophy is brought down from heaven: she was not engaged there in the free activities of leisure but was simply wasting her time in idleness. Now she is doing what is proper to her, the work and labor of human life.

Montaigne is one with his work. He tells us that his purpose requires that he write the *Essays* "at home, in a backward region." There, no one knows enough Latin or French to correct him. He says: "I would have done it better elsewhere, but the work would have been less my own; and its principal end and perfection is to be precisely my own" (VS875, F667). The work is completely at one with the author. This is the truth of the essays: "I have no more made my book than my book has made me—a book consubstantial with its author, concerned with my own self, an integral part of my life; not concerned with some third-hand, extraneous purpose, like all other books" (VS665, F504). He himself is "essays in flesh and bone" (VS844, F640).

Bringing himself into being and bringing the essays into being are not different actions. His is the first and only work to capture the fully authentic human being: "Authors communicate with the people by some special extrinsic mark; I am the first to do so by my entire being, as Michel de Montaigne" (VS805, F611). His essays are authentic, "original," in the most perfect way because they are precisely and completely *The Essays of Michel de Montaigne*.

AUTHENTICITY AND INAUTHENTICITY

The authentic individual makes himself his end or project, elevating himself to the "self-creating process," which is the "higher sphere of the good," as Hegel puts it. The authentic individual is self-contained, complete within himself, and satisfied within himself, for he alone makes himself to be what he is. He has no need of other men for his moral being or his satisfaction. Montaigne surpasses "all modern examples" in his independence from others. "Those who know me, both above and below me, know whether they have ever seen a man less demanding of others. If I surpass all modern examples in this respect, it is no great wonder, for so many parts of my character contribute to it," especially "my very favorite qualities, idleness and freedom" (VS969, F740–41). With respect to indebtedness to others, he says: "I see no one freer and less indebted than I am up to this point. . . . There is no one who is more absolutely clear of any others." He tries to have "no express need of anyone" (VS968, F739–40). Authenticity, then, entails the hiddenness of greatness: greatness has become knowing how to belong to oneself, how to be strong in oneself without honor and recognition. The replacement of moral virtue with authenticity, therefore, is the disappearance of the gentlemen.

The individual who is weak, who is not "strong in himself," cannot raise the given to the "higher sphere of the good" through a process of self-creation. This individual is "free" to make his needs, not himself, his end. As Hegel explains, this human being, in his subjective freedom, has this right to make his needs his end: "We may ask at this point whether the human being has a right to set himself ends which are not based on freedom, but solely on the fact that the subject is a living being. The fact that he is a living being is not contingent, however, but in accordance with reason, and to that extent he has a right to make his needs his end."[14] He is free to pursue the good in his particularity, as "the concrete person who, as a *particular* person, as a totality of needs and a mixture of natural necessity and arbitrariness, is his own end."[15] The slave is left at the mercy of his passions, inclinations, and instincts, and cannot rise above the satisfaction of his needs.

There is, then, a new *hidden* hierarchy of the authentic and the inauthentic, strong and weak. Yet community and, in particular, moral community becomes impossible because the authentic individual does not need other individuals for the moral life, and the inauthentic individual has no possibility of raising himself to the process of self-creation that is now the moral life. There can be no moral community of the authentic and inauthentic. The authentic individual, who is complete in himself, and the inauthentic individual, who makes his needs his end, are the characters perfectly suited for life in the new liberal order, where the higher things are hidden and the lower things are brought out into the light, and where civility replaces the tradition as the social bond.

FOUR

———————

Civility

Suppressing the Human Self

Early modern European history was the moment when the civil character "received its classic expression in the *Essais* of Montaigne."[1] Montaigne presents us with "a reading of the human condition in which a man's life is understood as an adventure in personal self-enactment" springing from a "disposition or sentiment in favour of self-direction in conduct." Such a man is related to others on these terms, as the man who belongs to himself.[2] The *Essays* are the first act of self-conscious civility.

Civility is the bond among those who do not need each other for the good life. Civility, then, replaces the social bond of the tradition in the absence of the possibility of moral community. Montaigne's invention of civility resolves the conflict between masters and slaves by bringing into being a new character that transcends the dependent relationship of masters and slaves, creating a society of equals. The resolution of the conflict between masters and slaves, then, rests upon the destruction of traditional moral community. The occasion for the possibility of Montaigne's invention of civility was the Protestant Reformation, with its rejection of the authority of sacred tradition.

To say that Montaigne *invented* civility is to say that he saw this possibility in the fragments of the shattered world of classical-Christian civilization and gave these fragments a coherent philosophical foundation. He gave philosophical form to something not natural, not inevitable, but something new that could be brought out of the old, if it were made self-conscious. He took the fragments and made them into a new character. In giving philosophical expression to this possibility, he helped to effect it, for now it could be seen as something defined and concrete in the fog of the destruction of the old world. It could be seen as something great and noble coming out of the ruins of the tradition of the great and noble.

To say that civility is a *philosophical* invention is not to say that only the philosopher can be civil, but that the philosopher brings this possibility—this new way of life—into reality and offers it as a possibility to others. In displaying himself as the new civil character, Montaigne intends to change the *mores* of his culture. Mores are "unreflective." Therefore, reform cannot take place at the superficial level of new opinions. True reform must occur at the deepest level of unreflective mores. Therefore, the philosopher must use the moral sensibilities that are already familiar. That is why he writes the essays as he does: he does not make arguments to persuade the mind; he addresses the sensibilities directly by displaying his "ways of being," the new character of a man in the world of everyday life.

Montaigne, then, draws on the familiar moral sources of the classical-Christian tradition to form the civil character. The very possibility of the moralization of pride, the renunciation of the natural human self, and the voluntary dissolution of the self has its source in Christianity: "I desire to be dissolved, to be with Jesus Christ." The generosity of civility also has its source in classical notions of nobility and magnanimity: Montaigne finds intimations of civility in his examples of merciful princes throughout the *Essays*, especially in his portrayal of the civility of the Theban commander Epaminondas. Removed from the context of the whole of the tradition, these fragments are now subordinated to the philosophical project of reordering man to himself.

Civility is necessary in the new liberal order to replace the old morality, to replace the tradition as the social bond. Montaigne believes that the tradition has been an ineffective limit on political power: the standard of the common good is really the deception by which the strong dominate the weak. Since the invention of civility is the resolution of the natural conflict between masters and slaves, the meaning of civility can be set out in terms of the way in which the new character of civility eliminates the gentlemen and liberates the slaves.

Eliminating the Gentlemen: The Suppression of the Natural Desire for Mastery

Because a *civil* society is a society from which the political struggle over who should rule is eliminated, the suppression of the natural desire for mastery is the condition for civility. Civility is the moral character that keeps society depoliticized. Civility must be above politics if it is to be an effective limit on politics. Civility rises above politics primarily through the revaluation of public and private life and thus the revaluation of honor. Montaigne effects this revaluation through the reformation of mores: the strong must now find their satisfaction and their moral fulfillment in the social virtues of private life, while private life is freed from the shame of servility to become good for its own sake. The suppression of the natural desire for mastery and the preference for private life appear in the *Essays* in the character and mores that Montaigne displays: the separation of the man from the prince, the interiorization of honor, the deliberate preference for private life, and the privatization of conscience. Taken together, these radical departures from the tradition amount to the privatization of morality. And the privatization of morality means that there is no public standard of morality, there are no public standards of honor and shame, and therefore there is no possibility of moral community.

First, as we saw in chapter 2, Montaigne insists on the "clear separation" of the man from the prince. By nature, no man is entitled to rule: the natural superiority of one man over others is not justification for mastery. The new prince, then, is the unnatural master to whom all must submit and before whom all are equal. The man who happens to be the philosopher *must* himself submit to the prince like everyone else. He must "step down" (VS916, F699), disappear into the crowd, and show his submission.[3] Civility is the "moralization of pride." It comes into being in the moment when the philosopher is the first to lay down his arms, risking his life in an act of surrender and submission. He gives up his superiority, acknowledging the others as equals even though they are not.

Second, the submission of the great to the new master entails the interiorization of honor. The moralization of pride is an act of greatness, nobility, and generosity, but greatness, nobility, and generosity are hidden in the act of submission. This is a very different understanding of greatness, for it is greatness without honor, greatness that hides itself and must hide itself because of what it has become. To "know how to belong to oneself"—the greatest thing in the world—is to be complete in oneself and to have no need of honor and recognition. Civility is what greatness becomes when all submit to the new master. Civility is the way in which greatness, nobility, and generosity remain in the new order: they are just barely visible and can only be seen and identified by the man who understands what they are.

Therefore, the man whose pride has been moralized does not get the honor he deserves in the new order: he knows that he does not get and cannot get what he deserves, and he accepts this injustice freely. The honorable has to be hidden and unrecognized because no one may rival the absolute power of the master, no one may outshine the master. Further, although it is essential to the new liberal order, civility can have little public visibility and recognition, because the new liberal order requires the suppression and hiddenness of the "higher things" in the interest of equality. Honor can have no honor in the new order.

Third, the interiorization of honor entails the deliberate preference for private life. Public life is the arena of honor and glory, the arena in which the gentlemen compete in displaying greatness and vying for honor, especially the honor of ruling over others. Montaigne emphasizes, from the very beginning of the *Essays*, that he is presenting a merely private life: "This book was written in good faith, reader. It warns you from the outset that in it I have set myself no goal but a domestic and private one. I have had no thought of serving either you or my own glory" (VS3, F2). A hidden life is a life without honor: "I set forth a humble and inglorious life; that does not matter. You can tie up all moral philosophy with a common and private life just as well as with a life of richer stuff. Each man bears the entire form of the human condition" (VS805, F611). The moral life is lived as a private life, without glory and honor. The great man must renounce the right to rule and become a private man, like everyone else.

Montaigne does not seek his own good in public life. He loves a private life because it is his own choice, not because he is unfit for public life. He serves his prince more gaily because he does so by the free choice of his judgment and reason, without personal obligation (VS988, F756). His will is free because he does not seek his own interest. He is not pressed by any passion either of hate or of love toward the great, nor is his will bound by any personal obligation or private interest (VS792, F601).

This detachment from public life is what he recommends to the great. In his essay on the education of a young gentleman, he advises the young man's tutor to form the will of his pupil to be a very loyal, very affectionate, and very courageous servant of his prince, but not to attach himself to that prince by private obligation, an attachment that impairs one's freedom. The judgment of a man who owes a personal debt to the prince, who is bought and paid for, is less free because he is unwilling to criticize the master who has preferred him and raised him up above his fellows. This kind of favor will dazzle him and corrupt his freedom to speak his mind (VS155, F114). The man who seeks his good in politics "must live not so much according to himself as according to others, not according to what he proposes to himself but according to what others propose to him" (VS991, F758).

Montaigne transforms the meaning of honor from visibility in public occupations to the invisibility of the hidden actions "valued only by each man in himself" in the private space of his conscience (VS1018–19, F779). Montaigne says that political philosophy may condemn his choice of a private life. Although he knows that the most honorable occupation is to serve the public, he stays out of it on account of his conscience (VS952, F727). In fact, his very limited experience in public life has disgusted him, so that he holds firm against temptations toward ambition (VS992, F759). Montaigne's treatment of ambition presents it as a weak and humiliating thirst for honor. "Since we will not do so out of conscience, at least out of ambition let us reject ambition. Let us disdain this base and beggarly hunger for renown and honor which makes us grovel for it before all sorts of people . . . abjectly and at no matter how vile a price" (VS1023, F783). Therefore, he performs whatever public occupations he is given in "the most private manner" he can (VS795, F603).

Fourth, the privatization of conscience creates the space for the free exercise of the noble character of civility. The man who happens to be the philosopher submits to the new, invisible master, but his submission is a free act, and, as the authentic individual, he belongs to himself and is strong in himself. Civility is the moral disposition that allows him to navigate the treacherous passage between submission and freedom of conscience in the new liberal order and to find his moral fulfillment in private life.

Montaigne was trusted by both sides in the civil wars of his day and served as negotiator between rival princes. In "Of the Useful and the Honorable" he describes the "innocence" of his conduct as negotiator between princes: "If anyone follows and watches me closely, I will concede him the victory if he does not confess that there is no rule in their school that could reproduce this natural movement and maintain a picture of liberty and license so constant and inflexible on such tortuous and varied paths, and that all their attention and ingenuity could not bring them to it" (VS795, F603). His constant and inflexible freedom might be described as his "integrity." There is "no rule" in any school of philosophy that can capture the consistency of his conduct, because this is his new moral character, which is not easily recognized.

In his presentations of the limits of what he will do in the service of his prince, Montaigne shows how his conscience is formed by the requirements of the trust and loyalty to his fellow citizens that constitute the social bond. He contrasts his observance of these limits with the practice of those ancients whose country "possessed and commanded their entire will" (VS1015, F777). He counsels this restraint with respect to the performance of those vicious actions that are necessary for the survival of one's country. If such actions become "excusable" because of necessity, "we still must let this part be played by the more vigorous and less fearful citizens, who sacrifice their honor and their conscience, as those ancients sacrificed their life, for the good [*salut*] of their country" (VS791, F600). Therefore, his service to the prince is "limited and conditional." There are princes, he says, "who do not accept men halfway and scorn limited and conditional services. There is no remedy. I frankly tell them my limits. . . .

And they too are wrong to demand of a free man the same subjection and obligation to their service as they demand of a man whom they have made and bought, or whose fortune is particularly and expressly attached to theirs" (VS794, F603). So he acknowledges the necessity of these ignoble actions, but he himself will not do them. He would not, he says, betray a private person for the prince (VS792, F600), and he does "not want to be considered either so affectionate or so loyal a servant as to be found fit to betray anyone." Nor will he knowingly lie for the prince (VS794, F603). The actions of those who betray and lie for the king are not only low; such persons "also prostitute [their] conscience" (VS799, F606). Montaigne does not allow his entire will to be possessed and commanded by his service to his prince: he is a man of integrity, and he belongs to himself. He is a partisan in the wars that divide his country, but his integrity is above partisanship. This transcendence of partisanship is an essential element of the civil character.

Montaigne also reluctantly served two terms as mayor of Bordeaux. In his description of his own actions as mayor, he shows us that the honorable is often about what we will *not* do. What we refrain from doing does not appear until and unless it is put in its proper light. It is just barely visible, and only to those who understand what it is. He emphasizes the fact that he often refrained from certain actions because he did not seek his own interest or his own glory in carrying out the duties of that office. These are the actions that have to be noticed and lifted *out of obscurity* and brought into the light *for their own sake* (VS1023, F783). These actions are "for their own sake" because they are without honor. Civility is what the nobility of the "for its own sake" has become in the new liberal order of equality.

Since the honorable is so often about hidden actions of restraint, throughout the *Essays* Montaigne focuses on the avoidance of vices, a focus in accord with his description of his reformation as "unlearning evil." The evil to be unlearned is the tradition of honor, especially the honor of avenging insults. The fact that he judges cruelty to be the worst of all vices shows that he regards the inclination to revenge as one of the chief obstacles to the elimination of the gentlemen.

In *Montaigne and the Quality of Mercy*, David Quint argues that the *Essays* reveal Montaigne's shifting attitude toward a model of heroic selfhood.[4] The *Essays* are directed to his noble contemporaries, especially at the vice of cruelty, which is so deeply associated with valor in combat. An ethical reform of his class is at the heart of his political project: true nobility is displayed in the determination to avoid cruelty. Quint argues persuasively that by making clemency the supreme expression of true valor, Montaigne substitutes clemency for valor as the distinguishing sign of aristocratic identity.[5] Indeed, "the choice of pardon over revenge is the moral and political touchstone of the *Essais*."[6] In his chapter entitled "An Ethics of Yielding," Quint describes Montaigne's moral teaching as an ethics of submission that shows the nobility how to yield while retaining honor and integrity.[7] This is "an honorable kind of submission that is the result of free individual choice."[8]

Montaigne first appears in the essays as the man who might possibly be the conquering prince. If he were such a prince, he would be easily moved by both esteem for the naturally strong and pity for the naturally weak. The Stoics hold that pity is "a vicious passion," but Montaigne is naturally moved by pity, for he is "marvelously weak in the direction of mercy and gentleness" (VS8, F4). This fundamental preference for mercy—displayed in the very first essay—is developed through the entire work. Montaigne ranks cruelty as the worst of all vices: "Among other vices, I cruelly hate cruelty, both by nature and by judgment, as the extreme of all vices" (VS429, F313). Although cruelty had always been regarded as a vice in both classical and Christian morality, he is the first philosopher to claim that it is the extreme of all vice.

Montaigne's ranking of cruelty as the extreme of vice appears to come from the Christian aspects of the tradition. Although he says that the *Essays* are entirely human, with "no admixture of theology" (VS322, F234), there is one instance in which he does, in fact, call upon the help of theology. In "Of Cruelty" he defends his sympathy with the animals, a sympathy that makes him appear weak. His hatred of cruelty verges on extreme "softness" and is therefore easily mistaken for weakness, so he must defend himself against the ridicule that might come from this appearance of weakness: "And so that people will not laugh at this sympathy that I have with [animals], Theology herself orders us to show some favor in their regard; and considering that one and the same master has lodged us in this place for his service, and that they, like ourselves, are of his family, she is right to enjoin upon us some respect and affection toward them" (VS433, F316).

Montaigne's father had sent him to the poorest village in his neighborhood to be nursed and had him held over the baptismal font by villagers of the lowest condition in order to attach and oblige him to them. "His plan," Montaigne says, "succeeded not at all badly. I give myself willingly to the little people, whether because there is more glory in it, or through natural compassion, which has infinite power over me" (VS1100, F844). By associating his compassion with his baptism, he points to the Christian origin of this element of his disposition. By mentioning the motivation of glory, he points to classical magnanimity. Both of these sources from the tradition support the "infinite power" of his natural compassion and his "marvelous weakness" in the direction of mercy and gentleness.

The components of civility that come to light in Montaigne's "elimination of the gentlemen" are his integrity, his carelessness of honor and recognition, and his compassion, mercy, and gentleness toward the weak. When Montaigne studies the ancient histories, he finds intimations of civility and the suppression of the natural desire for mastery. In the Theban general Epaminondas, he sees the beginnings of the possibility of the separation of the man from the prince and the preference for private life. Epaminondas was the commander who led the Thebans to victory over the Spartans and freed Thebes from the domination of Sparta at the battle of Leuctra in 371 BC. Plutarch's life of Epaminondas has not survived, and even though Cicero refers to him as "the first man of Greece," very little remains of the writings about him.[9] Montaigne's portrait of Epaminondas is consistent with the ancient sources, but he also "probes the inside" and invents the "springs of action" in his interpretation of the histories (VS338, F244). Epaminondas was a great and fearless warrior. Although he has not nearly as much glory as Alexander or Caesar, his resolution and valor are equal to theirs. But his "character and conscience" far surpassed all those who have ever undertaken to manage affairs. "For in this respect, which must be principally considered, which alone truly marks what we are, and which I weigh alone against all the others together," he is the most outstanding man who ever lived (VS756, F573).

The character and conscience of Epaminondas, which make him superior to Alexander and Caesar, are seen most clearly in his refusal to put aside his "private duty" even at the risk of failing in his greatest enterprises. He raised consideration for his private duty to such a height that he never killed a man he had conquered, and was reluctant to kill a tyrant, even when the liberty of his country was at stake (VS802, F609). He showed "humanity" even toward enemy forces (VS756, F574). In the midst of battle, "this man was not even kept from hearing the voices of civility and pure courtesy" (VS802, F609).

Epaminondas teaches us that "the common interest must not require all things of all men against the private interest . . . and that not all things are permissible for an honorable man in the service of his king or of the common cause, or of the laws" (VS802, F609). Honor and greatness, then, are now seen in a very different light: "If it is greatness of heart and the effect of rare and singular virtue to despise friendship, private obligations, our word, and kinship, for the common good and obedience to the magistrate, truly it is enough to excuse us from this that it is a greatness that cannot lodge in the greatness of Epaminondas' heart" (VS802, F609–10). The character and conscience of Epaminondas reveal the meaning of true greatness and the meaning of civility in the refusal to use any and all means in the pursuit of political goals.

Montaigne concludes his portrait of Epaminondas with the observation that "the prosperity of his country died, as it was born, with him" (VS757, F574). That the freedom and prosperity of Thebes depended entirely on the character and ability of Epaminondas is a fact noted by the ancient historians as well. As Epaminondas lay dying, he ordered the Thebans to make peace, because they had no one left to lead them.[10] Cornelius Nepos concludes his life of Epaminondas with a "comment about his character and life, a comment no one can dispute. Before Epaminondas was born and after he died Thebes was the satellite of a foreign power. But while he directed the state, Thebes was the most powerful city in Greece. From this fact anyone can see that Epaminondas as an individual was mightier than the whole state."[11]

It is Machiavelli who explains why Thebes did not remain free after the death of Epaminondas. Even though Thebes was a "corrupt" city on account of the idleness of the oligarchs, Epaminondas was able to turn the Theban peasants into a fierce army and to accomplish an extraordinary victory over the Spartans.[12] But when Epaminondas died, Thebes came under the power of Philip of Macedon.[13] Machiavelli concludes that a virtuous man such as Epaminondas cannot live long enough to transform a city from bad to good. His city "is ruined, unless indeed he makes it to be reborn with many dangers and much blood. For such corruption and slight aptitude for free life arise from an inequality that is in that city; and if one wishes to make it equal, it is necessary to use the greatest extraordinary means, which few know how or wish to use."[14]

The extraordinary means to which Machiavelli refers is the elimination of the idle and rich oligarchs. "Those are called gentlemen who live idly in abundance from the returns of their possessions without having any care either for cultivation or for other necessary trouble in living. Such as these are pernicious in every republic and in every province. . . . In these provinces no republic or political way of life has ever emerged for such kinds of men are altogether hostile to every civilization." Machiavelli draws this conclusion: "He who wishes to make a republic where there are very many gentlemen cannot do it unless he first eliminates all of them."[15] "Gentlemen," which had been a term of honor, has now become a pejorative term: the noble gentlemen have become the idle rich, who are hostile to civilization, and "civilization" is now a condition of equality.

Epaminondas shows what civility is when "the voice of civility" calls him to turn from his glorious deeds as a prince to his "humanity" in sparing his friend. But from Machiavelli's perspective, the "problem" with Epaminondas is precisely his "humanity." He could not do what needed to be done, for he could not bring himself to eliminate the oligarchs. Montaigne is actually doing something greater than Epaminondas, for he *does* eliminate the gentlemen, by nonviolent means—that is, by transforming mores through the revaluing of honor and greatness. His reformation of mores is the "clear separation" of the man from the prince (in representative government), the interiorization of the honorable, and the privatization of morality, thus erasing the possibility of moral community and forming the gentlemen for life in civil society.

LIBERATING THE SLAVES: EMBRACING UNNATURAL EQUALITY

Liberating the slaves means freeing the realm of work and labor from its hiddenness and shame and freeing the worker and the laborer from his subjection to the requirements of the common good within the hierarchical structure of the tradition, so that each is free to pursue the good in his own way. However, the price of this new freedom is the submission of all to the *new* master: modern society is the association of equals because it is the result of the submission of all to this new master. Recall Hobbes's ninth law of nature, the law against pride: since no one will enter the agreement to submit to the master except on equal terms, each man must acknowledge the others as his equals even though they are not equal by nature. In the presence of the master, all are equally slaves.

Because there must be no struggle for rule in the social realm, the condition of civility is the only way in which society can remain depoliticized: the freedom of society is freedom from the political. It is in this sense that civility can be said to be "above" politics: it keeps society free of the conflict between masters and slaves, strong and weak.

The traditional moral virtues, which have their existence in the political community of the city, are now replaced by the "social virtues" that constitute civility. Civility is the quality that elevates the relationships among free individuals in society above the merely servile and useful, making them free. Civility makes their everyday interactions good "for their own sake." To put it differently, civility is the moral component of social life. That is why we can speak of the "moralization" of pride: only the man whose pride has been moralized can participate in a society of equals.

Since society is the free association of equals in which each seeks the good in his particularity, civil society is not moral community. The idea of civil society, as Michael Oakeshott explains, is that of agents who are joined not by the bond of a common substantive purpose or common interest but only by a bond of "loyalty to one another." This loyalty is expressed in the agreement to acknowledge the authority of the laws that specify only the conditions for acting, not a substantive good.[16] But law itself is not enough to maintain this loyalty: there must be a more fundamental disposition to live under laws, to accept the authority of the laws even though they are imperfect and unjust, and to live with others as equals under the law even though they are not equal. This disposition is civility. Therefore, civility itself cannot be legislated, for it is the moral character that is the condition for this loyalty to one another.[17]

Civility, then, operates in the space where the law is silent. It covers the interactions where the law does not reach. In this way, civility elevates social relationships above the level of the coercive power of the law. This is the space where private judgment is exercised and where conscience has freedom and authority.

The features of the new character of civility reveal the way in which the authentic individual forms himself for life in the new liberal order. In particular, we can uncover the natural passions, instincts, and inclinations that must be encouraged or suppressed in the man whose pride has been "moralized." These are especially the movements of the soul in its natural desire for honor and recognition. Civility is what greatness becomes in the renunciation of pride and the acknowledgment and acceptance of unnatural equality.

The most fundamental reform of mores that must occur if individuals are to acknowledge each other as equals is the reformation of judgment itself. Because morality has become a private concern and because it is impossible to tell from the "outside" whether another man is authentic or not, the way in which human beings judge each other is crucial for the attitude of civility. Montaigne judges both himself and all other men as incommensurable particulars. That is, he does not judge by a universal standard of perfection, for there is no common human nature and no common measure. Nor does he judge others by the standard of himself. This is a true reformation of mores: changing the way we judge ourselves and each other at the most fundamental level.

The ability to judge oneself as an incommensurable particular is captured in Pierre Manent's discussion of the way Montaigne compares himself to other men and the way in which his own self-esteem does not depend on comparison with others. Because he belongs to himself, Montaigne can acknowledge the loftiness of Cato, for example, without envy or resentment: "Comparison, when it takes place, is done by a man who is so calm and confident in his own form that he considers the other forms of life with a gaze that is free of all rivalry, free of all resentment."[18] By the standard of natural perfection, others are superior or inferior to him. Thus, the new standard of equality is not natural: by the nonnatural standard of self-possession, he is unique. Montaigne values himself at his true worth. He has renounced the naïve self-esteem of the traditional hierarchy in order see himself as he is and to form himself by himself. The new kind of self-esteem does not depend upon others for recognition but depends entirely upon his own recognition that he alone has made himself to be what he is.

Descartes's treatment of the virtue of generosity in the *Passions of the Soul* can help us to understand the way Montaigne judges himself and others. Descartes says that we can acquire the virtue of generosity by *reflection* on our own thoughts and wills.[19] This is the transformation of oneself that occurs entirely within oneself through reflection that is the doubleness that is the condition for knowledge of ourselves and for self-reformation.

For Descartes, true generosity consists in the knowledge that nothing belongs to us but the freedom of the will and in the resolution to undertake and carry out whatever we judge to be best.[20] Generosity, then, causes us to esteem ourselves in accordance with our true value, but it also has to do with our judgment of others. "Those who possess this knowledge and this feeling about themselves readily come to believe that any other person can have the same knowledge and feeling about himself, *because this involves nothing which depends on someone else.* That is why such people never have contempt for anyone." Rather, they excuse others because "they suppose [a virtuous will] also to be present, or at least capable of being present, in every other person."[21] This is the way Montaigne approaches every other human being, excusing weakness and supposing the presence of a virtuous will.

Civility flows from the way he looks at others and judges others. Since morality is private and hidden, the bond of civility must be something that respects the privacy of morality, that does not make substantive judgments about the way others live: "A sound intellect will refuse to judge men simply by their outward actions" (VS338, F244). The generous man decides to assume the presence of a virtuous will in everyone, "as if" every individual is acting in good faith.

The elements of civility flow from this generosity of judgment: promise keeping, forgiveness of insults, openness, toleration, and trust. All are about respecting the individual in his particularity and in his right to the satisfaction of his particularity.

The bond that unites incommensurable particulars in civil society is the loyalty pledged in the promise that is the expression and binding of the will. "Since mutual understanding is brought about solely by way of the word, he who falsifies it betrays human society. It is the only instrument by means of which our wills and thoughts communicate, it is the interpreter of our soul. If it fails us, we have no more hold on each other, no more knowledge of each other. If it deceives us, it breaks up all our relations and dissolves all the bonds of our society" (VS666, F505). Lying is a most destructive vice, because "we are men and hold together only by our word" (VS36, F23).

In a passage that anticipates Hobbes, Montaigne writes of "false and lax rules" in philosophy: if robbers have seized you and have set you free again after extracting from you a promise to pay a ransom, it is wrong to say that an honest man will be excused from keeping his word once he is out of their power. "Nothing of the sort. What fear has once made me will, I am bound still to will when without fear. . . . Otherwise we shall come by degrees to overthrow all the rights that a third person obtains from our promises and oaths. *As if force can be brought to bear on a brave man* [Cicero]" (VS801, F608). The promise to keep the laws can be motivated by fear, as it is for most men, or by the courage and generosity of the proud. As Hobbes tells us, the "nobleness of courage" is "rarely found,"[22] and the generosity of the proud is "a generosity too rarely found to be presumed upon."[23] Civility must begin or originate in the rare generosity of the proud—the moralization of pride—but the example that Montaigne presents in the *Essays* shows the "ease" of this disposition and its accessibility to all human beings: it is not limited to the nobility in the traditional sense.

In *The Human Condition*, Hannah Arendt gives an account of human action that shows how promise keeping is joined with forgiveness to make social interaction enduring. "The possible redemption from the predicament of irreversibility—of being unable to undo what one has done though one did not, and could not, have known what he was doing—is the faculty of forgiving. The remedy for unpredictability, for the chaotic uncertainty of the future, is contained in the faculty to make and keep promises." These two faculties must be present together "in so far as one of them, forgiving, serves to undo the deeds of the past, whose 'sins' hang like Damocles' sword over every new generation; and the other, binding oneself through promises, serves to set up in the ocean of uncertainty, which is the future by definition, islands of security without which not even continuity, let alone durability of any kind, would be possible in the relations between men."[24]

Forgiveness—the constant will to forgiveness—is necessary because human freedom is such that men "trespass" against each other every day. These "everyday" trespasses are not crimes (which must be punished) but simply the give-and-take of free individuals, each pursuing the good in his own way. "Trespassing is an everyday occurrence which is in the very nature of action's constant establishment of new relationships within a web of relations, and it needs forgiving, dismissing, in order to make it possible for life to go on by constantly releasing men from what they have done unknowingly. Only through this constant mutual release from what they do can men remain free agents."[25] Forgiveness is necessary for civil association precisely on account of the presupposition of both human imperfection and human freedom. Indeed, the nature of freedom makes imperfection inevitable and, in a certain sense, acceptable.

Because the laws do not claim to be just, civility means accepting the fact that you do not get the honor you deserve. Montaigne says that "among men, as soon as an altercation over precedence in walking or sitting goes beyond three replies, it is *uncivil*. I have no fear of ceding or preceding unfairly to avoid such a bothersome argument, and never did a man covet my right to go first but that I yielded it to him" (VS980, F749, emphasis added). One of the principal consolations that he has for his deficient memory is that he does not even remember injuries received (VS35, F23). "Vengeance is a sweet passion, whose impact is great and natural: I see this well enough, though I have no experience of it in myself" (VS835, F634).

As Arendt says, "The discoverer of the role of forgiveness in the realm of human affairs was Jesus of Nazareth."[26] Forgiveness is "the exact opposite of vengeance," and "the freedom contained in Jesus' teaching of forgiveness is the freedom from vengeance."[27] The essential role of forgiveness shows the way in which the possibility of civility depends on the fragments of Christian moral teaching. This is not to say that mercy was not practiced in pre-Christian societies—Montaigne gives many examples of this—but that vengeance can no longer be seen as honorable.

The transformation of greatness required for civility is further expressed in the following claim by Montaigne: "If my heart is not great enough, it is compensatingly open, and it orders me boldly to publish its weakness" (VS917, F700). In a society of equals, greatness becomes openness. And the fact that he reveals his weakness shows that this openness is not about honor and recognition of superior strength. Openness compensates for greatness: classical magnanimity has become the generosity of openness, which is, first and foremost, self-revelation. "A generous heart should not belie its thoughts; it wants to reveal itself even to its inmost depths. There everything is good, or at least everything is human" (VS647, F491).

The virtue of civility can be brought out more clearly in its similarities to and differences from the classical virtue of magnanimity. Magnanimity is the culmination of the moral virtues and is thus the highest level that classical morality can reach. The philosophical description of the magnanimous or great-souled man occurs in the *Ethics*, where Aristotle goes through the list of virtues and defines each in relation to its two opposite vices, one of excess and one of deficiency. In Aristotle's description, the great-souled man is actually defined in terms of the attitude he has toward honor, as, for example, the courageous man is defined in terms of his attitude toward fear. The great-souled man thinks he deserves and truly does deserve great things. The greatest of the "external goods" and the prize of the noblest achievements is honor, so the great-souled man regards himself as worthy of honor. The magnanimous man does not need honor, and he certainly will not grovel for it, but he is justifiably proud, and he does not hide but rather displays his superiority in great and noble deeds.[28]

In the *Essays*, self-revelation is transformed from the public visibility of shining noble actions—which needs no words—to the exposure of common, ordinary weakness. Custom has made speaking about oneself a vice on account of the temptation to boastfulness, but speaking about oneself is actually the cure for pride (VS379, F274). Montaigne uncovers himself, revealing the most private aspects of his life. This is the act of generosity that lies at the origin of society. Montaigne has made the first generous gesture. What he reveals is not his strength but his weakness, the lowest and most common aspects of his humanity. What he conceals is the honorable act of the courage and generosity of his self-effacement. That is how civility takes magnanimity a step further.

Pierre Manent explains how the magnanimous man of Aristotle is very different from the generous man of Montaigne. "The generous heart of Montaigne thus appears as a strange mixture of Greek magnanimity, which claims before its fellow citizens the honors due its noble actions, and the contrite Christian who confesses his bad actions before God." However, "by taking away from the generosity about which he is speaking everything that concerns action and the honors due to noble actions, Montaigne profoundly changes the notion of magnanimity." At the same time, he does not confess his sins but rather reveals what is merely human, his human weakness.[29]

Self-revelation is essential to the social bond. Dissimulation, or hiding oneself under a mask, testifies to cowardice and baseness of heart: "In that way our men train for perfidy; being accustomed to speak false words, they have no scruples about breaking their word." Referring to the practices of the nobles at court, Montaigne writes: "As for this new virtue of hypocrisy and dissimulation, which is so highly honored at present, I mortally hate it: and of all vices, I know none that testifies to so much cowardice and baseness of heart" (VS647, F491). Through his openness he wants to encourage the nobility to attain freedom by rising above cowardice and hypocrisy (VS845, F642). It requires courage to speak of oneself (VS664, F503), while "not to speak roundly of oneself shows some lack of heart" (VS942, F720). It is craven and servile to disguise and hide ourselves, and not to dare to show ourselves as we are.

Openness is a kind of transparency that displays itself in his demeanor: "I have an open way that easily insinuates itself and gives credit on first acquaintance. Pure naturalness and truth, in whatever age, still find their time and place. . . . My freedom has also freed me easily from any suspicion of dissimulation by its vigor. . . . I am not pressed by any passion either of hate or of love toward the great, nor is my will bound by personal injury or obligation. . . . This is what makes me walk everywhere head high, face and heart open" (VS792, F600–601).

As Manent insists, "No one has gone toward others with so much confidence—'trust'—one that is not naïve, but on the contrary, quite deliberate . . . . It is a matter of going toward others, who are always threatening, without putting oneself on the defensive, but on the contrary, exposing oneself. If there is a formulation that sums up the disposition, the attitude, the procedure of Montaigne among his fellow human beings, it is certainly *with an open face*."[30]

The risk of openness and of promise keeping is possible only on condition of trust. The existence of a civil, free society depends upon trust. "Trust becomes necessary in the face of the free, autonomous, and hence unknowable individual. This self-regarding individual stands at the source of the new terms of civility and friendship that define the modern age." The need for trust made the idea of the "promise" central to early modern political theory. A civil society requires a shared belief in the act of promise keeping. "It is only when agency, in the freedom of promise keeping, can come to play a major role that trust must also come to play a part in defining interpersonal relations. Trust is not only a means of negotiating risk; it implies risk"—namely, the risk "inherent in the other person's agency."[31]

The openness and generosity of the civil disposition are especially important for the practice of freedom of speech. Freedom of speech is essential for the preservation of a society that is civil, because communication, as the revelation of particularity, is essential to the social bond. Montaigne describes himself as open to all opinions and to heated discussion.

> I do not at all hate opinions contrary to mine. I am so far from being vexed to see discord between my judgments and others', and from making myself incompatible with the society of men because they are of a different sentiment and party from mine, that on the contrary, since variety is the most general fashion that nature has followed, and more in minds than bodies. . . . I find it much rarer to see our humors and designs agree. And there were never in the world two opinions alike, any more than two hairs or grains. Their most universal quality is diversity." (VS785–86, F597–98)

The most important and most valuable diversity is diversity of minds.

In "Of the Art of Discussion" he elaborates on the attitudes that free speech requires. "I enter into discussion and argument with great freedom and ease, inasmuch as opinion finds in me a bad soil to penetrate and take deep roots in. No propositions astonish me, no belief offends me, whatever contrast it offers with my own" (VS923, F704). He is not offended nor does he respond with anger: "So contradictions of opinions neither offend nor affect me; they merely arouse and exercise me. . . . When someone opposes me, he arouses my attention, not my anger" (VS924, F705). This "verbal jousting" is "the sharp repartee which high spirits and familiarity introduce among friends," which Manent characterizes as "the only satisfactory and complete response" to the social situation of comparison.[32]

Montaigne associates the inability to converse in this manner with a tyrannical disposition: "It is always a tyrannical ill humor to be unable to endure a way of thinking different from your own" (VS928, F709). In fact, in what may be the only instance in the *Essays* where he refers to himself as perfect, he says with respect to bantering and joking: "I am perfect in forbearance, for I endure retaliation, not only sharp but even indiscreet, without being disturbed" (VS938, F717). Again, we see in the openness and good humor of his speech the stance of the individual who is above the rancor of partisanship.

All of the features of civility are embodied in the *Essays*. The *Essays*, then, are themselves the first display of self-conscious civility, not only because of what they say but also because of what they do in the act of generous self-revelation.

SOCIABLE WISDOM

The man who happens to be the philosopher desires to reveal himself and discovers to his astonishment that he is a new figure of the philosopher, an unpremeditated and accidental philosopher. Unpremeditated and accidental philosophy is "sociable wisdom" (VS1116, F857), the philosopher's participation in society, the act of self-revelation that is the social bond. Sociable wisdom makes social life civil, elevating it above the merely servile.

In taking the stance of the detached observer, the philosopher empties himself of his particularity as a man and ceases to be a participant in the social order. He hides himself, his originality, and his strength so that the new order can be brought into the light. The *Essays* are Montaigne's recovery of his particularity and his return to the world of men as a participant, but in a very different way from how the classical philosopher revealed his particularity and participated in the natural hierarchy of the old order.

The openness, generosity, and toleration of the newly civilized man are manifest in the testing of himself in conversation with the philosophers, poets, and historians of the tradition. At the same time, Montaigne's style (as Pascal describes it) is "totally composed of thoughts born out of the ordinary conversations of life."[33] Montaigne transforms the thoughts of ordinary conversation into unpremeditated and accidental philosophy. Philosophy disappears into the practice of everyday life, while the new man reveals himself in his concrete particularity, satisfying the desire in which philosophy began. Philosophy begins in the renunciation of particular desire in all of its personal concreteness, but it ends in the enjoyment of the philosopher's new particularity that he has achieved in his reappropriation of the natural man.

Philosophy is barely visible in the *Essays*. It is hidden in the stance that he takes on himself and the world, the stance of the invisible observer, the stance of reflection. Philosophy must be hidden as merely unpremeditated and accidental, as sociable wisdom, because nothing can appear to be higher than the prince and because the philosopher must participate in society as an equal. The particular man who happens to be the philosopher submits to the pure human will, like everyone else. Montaigne says that the advantage of greatness is that "it can step down whenever it pleases, and that it almost has the choice of both conditions," of greatness or lowliness (VS916, F699), while the disadvantage of greatness is the difficulty of enjoying the greatest pleasure of common life. "There is perhaps nothing more pleasant in association with men than the trials [*essais*] of strength we have with one another, in rivalry of honor and worth, whether in exercises of the body or of the mind" (VS918, F701). The great cannot share in this pleasure on account of the fear and awe that their power inspires in others: they cannot compete in this rivalry on equal terms. "Stepping down" into the social, then, makes this essaying of oneself possible and easy.

In the essays of strength in rivalry of honor and worth, Montaigne is the strongest and greatest, for he has performed the most bold, daring,

and difficult act of all in overturning the ancient hierarchy and transforming the very meaning of honor and worth. The ancient *agon*—the
struggle for recognition of superiority—is transformed into the peaceful
essaying of civil men.

Philosophy becomes play, and the freedom of philosophy is the freedom not of leisure but of play. Philosophy is the play of possibility, the
freedom of the mind to bring the new out of the old. The trials of strength
are sport, not the serious rivalry for recognition and the right to rule that
characterizes the struggles within the ancient city.

Aristotle distinguishes leisure from play. Play resembles leisure because play seems to have no end outside itself, but while leisure is concerned with noble and serious things, play is merely "charming dexterity."
That is why tyrants enjoy having playful people around them: "They
make themselves pleasant in the very things that tyrants are after, and
such are the sorts of people tyrants need."[34] Tyrants are the enemies of
leisure: they fear those who are noble and serious because such men are
not slavish. But the new master has nothing to fear from the philosopher
who describes his project as "a new and extraordinary amusement"
(VS378, F273) and his subject as "vain and frivolous" (VS3, F2).

Sociable wisdom is the ongoing suppression of the philosopher's
natural superiority, bringing civility out of natural inequality and pride.
Without the philosophical virtue of civility, the natural conflict between
masters and slaves cannot be suppressed, society cannot remain depoliticized, and the power and force of the rule of the master are naked. The
philosophical virtue of civility covers over that naked power and force.

FIVE

The Deterioration of Civility

When Everything Becomes Political

The failure of civility teaches us what is necessary for the preservation of civility. It shows us that a civil society must preserve institutions and practices that are free from the conflicts of politics. When "everything is political," civility becomes impossible. In this chapter, I will discuss the deterioration of free institutions, especially the universities, and the suppression of free speech in both public life and the universities.

As I have argued, only a depoliticized society can be a free, *civil* society. Montaigne's description of the education of a free individual emphasizes the preparation of the student for a self-directed life that requires independent judgment based primarily on the study of philosophy and history. In other words, he recognizes the importance of the study of the tradition as the background for good judgment. He also celebrates the practice of free discussion as one of the great pleasures of human life and as an essential freedom in a civil society. The failure of civility that we lament today can be traced in good part to the politicization of education and to the stifling effects of "politically correct" speech both on our campuses and in our public life.

Civility is the social bond in the liberal order of state and society, in which the state is the power of coercion and society is the space of the freedom of individuals to pursue the good, each in his own way. The failure of civility is the reemergence of the conflict of masters and slaves into the social sphere, the willingness to effect the intrusion of the state into the free association of individuals. Because the power and authority of the state are absolute (only the state can determine when and how it should interfere in society) the maintenance of a free society requires self-imposed restraint on the part of the citizens to resist bringing the power of the state to bear in the social sphere.

Civility operates in the spaces where the law is silent and therefore gives room for the exercise of individual choice. Civility is necessary for a free society, and a free society is necessary for the practice of civility. Edward Shils argues that societies that do not allow individual freedom also live without a sense of civil affinity, for civility is "shriveled and shrunken by fear" of the coercive power of the state.[1]

In his discussion of "the totalitarian temptation," Roger Scruton describes a totalitarian government as "one that does not respect or acknowledge the distinction between civil society and State."[2] Society serves as the limit on the power of government by preserving the intermediate sources of authority that the state has a tendency to crush. Civil society consists of institutions that hedge about the power of the state and presupposes a government of limited powers. Civil society also requires free institutions that are not only permitted to remain independent of government control but that define the limits of the power of the government, especially the moral, religious, intellectual, and economic institutions that have authority and autonomy and that, at the same time, foster the virtue of civility. If the state oppresses and suppresses these free institutions, then there is no civil society. "A totalitarian society is the antithesis of civil society."[3]

Free institutions foster and preserve civility *because* they foster and preserve tradition. They keep alive those fragments of the tradition that are higher than politics and that are necessary for the practice of civility, which must be a free act and cannot be coerced or legislated. Shils explains the role of the social institutions of family, church, and university: "This combination of institutions inculcating moral and intellectual beliefs is the foundation of the trans-temporal and trans-local structure of society. These institutions provide the internal spine and the outer frame of the culture which maintains a society. Where they fail to do so, the society is in danger of losing its character as a society. It becomes disordered in its present organization through the loss of the constraints imposed on its present by its past."[4] Civility deteriorates when tradition is replaced by ideology and the universities are no longer the guardians of tradition.

FREE INSTITUTIONS AND PRACTICES

Society becomes politicized when tradition is replaced by ideology. In his discussion of "tradition and the rationalization of societies," Shils explains that modern societies, especially in the West, "have cultivated, in many forms, ideals which are, explicitly or implicitly, directly or indirectly, injurious to substantive tradition . . . , 'dynamic' ideals . . . which require active and deliberate movement away from substantive traditional patterns of belief and action. The dynamic ideals are not ideals of heroism; they are ideals which entail rationality in the application of abstract principles. . . . The 'dynamic' ideal in Western societies requires departures from traditional ways of seeing and doing things. It is an expression of discontent with what has been received."[5]

Ideology is an attempt to reconstitute a coherent whole to replace the tradition in which man is ordered to the divine. Ideology is the coherent whole in which man is ordered to man. Tradition is replaced by political "ideals," the ideals of equality and freedom. As Richard Rorty tells us, "The ideals of the Enlightenment" are "our most precious cultural heritage," and "the preservation of the values of the Enlightenment is our best hope."[6] Ideals are not naturally given ends. Rather, ideals are creations of philosophy, "possibilities" invented by the philosophical mind. Therefore they have no natural limits: there is no end, only becoming and change. For Rorty, the realization of utopia is "an endless process—an endless, proliferating realization of Freedom."[7]

Ideology introduces political conflict into society, because ideology justifies the illegitimate imposition of the standard of a "common good" on a structure that depends upon the rejection of the common good. The "enlightened" seek to impose the ideology by force on the unenlightened. The ideal of "social justice" is precisely such an intrusion, requiring the state to interfere in every aspect of social life.

Shils defines ideology as the belief that "politics should be conducted from the standpoint of a coherent, comprehensive set of beliefs which must override every other consideration." Ideology, then, radiates into every sphere of life: it replaces religion and rules over philosophy and even family life. Ideological politics is an orientation toward an "ideal" with the conviction that the attainment of the ideal will institute a condition of perfection, a new order in which all of the evils of the existing system will have been overcome. Therefore, ideology breeds "a deep distrust of traditional institutions" (such as family, church, and schools) as the source of these evils and as obstacles to progress toward the ideal.[8] For ideological politics, the highest end is "a purified and perfected society."[9] Tradition, on the contrary, limits our expectations of what politics can do.

Michael Oakeshott describes a political ideology as an abstract principle or set of principles for determining what goals should be pursued by society as a whole. Sometimes this is a single abstract idea such as freedom or equality; sometimes it is a complex scheme of related ideas, such as democracy or Marxism. Those who see politics this way believe that an ideology can take the place of understanding the tradition of political behavior. But for Oakeshott, every political ideology is an abstraction from and therefore a distortion of a tradition of political activity.[10]

One of the most important differences between ideology and tradition is that tradition is not an idea or a system of ideas, but a way of life, a fundamental orientation of the whole person, his beliefs, sensibilities, sympathies. It is what Oakeshott calls "a flow of sympathy."[11] Shils describes tradition as "the 'tacit component' of rational, moral, and cognitive actions, and of affect."[12] Tradition can never be supplanted by calculation, reason, or power. It is not possible to maintain a social order based solely on force and coercion, for social order rests on those precontractual elements of solidarity whose source is the tradition.

Unlike ideology, tradition is not about ideals. Therefore, tradition is not concerned with attaining a condition of perfection and is not just about the future. But neither is it only about the past. The social bond, the sense of affinity on which civil politics rests, is not the work of the moment but connects us to those who have lived, are living, and will live within that bond.[13]

While it may seem that a strong sense of tradition within a civil society inhibits change, correction, and improvement, Shils claims that criticism, correction, and improvement of any institution require the context that is provided by tradition, because tradition provides an underlying stability. "Order is preserved by the integration of conflicting interests, the authority of tradition and law, and by leaving an area for the conflict of interests to work itself out freely."[14]

Shils notes that liberal democratic regimes place great burdens on the civil sense, because they permit open conflict and acknowledge and thus encourage partisanship. Teresa Bejan, in *Mere Civility: Disagreement and the Limits of Toleration*, explains: "As a regime, liberal democracy is distinguished by its dedication to *two-fold* toleration: (1) of diversity in its members' fundamental identities and commitments (especially in politics and religion) and (2) of the disagreements those differences inspire. Indeed, the self-conception of liberal societies as 'tolerant' hinges on the fact that members are not compelled to confine their differences to a private sphere of individual skulls or intimate familiars, but are permitted, even encouraged, to express them freely in public and to compete for adherents."[15]

Civility, however, requires a transcendence of partisanship. Montaigne exhibits this transcendence of partisanship throughout the *Essays* in his descriptions of his conduct in the religious and civil wars of his day. He is a member of the Catholic party, and he is willing to fight for its cause, but he is trusted by both sides and becomes a negotiator between the warring factions. As I have discussed in chapter 4, he places firm limits on what he will do and what he will not do in his service to his prince and his party: he will not lie and he will not betray any man. In other words, his integrity does not permit him to do anything and everything, to use any means necessary, to further the cause of his party. The social bond itself is higher than, more important than, the success of his political faction.

The criterion by which civil politics operates is a solicitude for the interest of the whole society. Civility, then, is "the concern for the maintenance of the civil society as a civil society"—that is, as a society of free

association of individuals.[16] Bejan describes civility as the minimum degree of courtesy required in social situations. "*Mere* civility [is] a minimal
conformity to norms of respectful behavior and decorum expected of all
members of a tolerant society as such."[17] But civility has to be more than
good manners: if there is not a more fundamental disposition to observe
good manners, then courtesy will wither away. Civility means that the individual exercises self-restraint in political conflict. If there is nothing
above politics, nothing more important than politics, then politics itself
cannot be civil. The civil individual is more concerned to preserve the
free association than to have his way in the political struggle.

In his "Trust, Confidence, and the Problem of Civility," Adam Seligman also shows the way civility assumes both the freedom of individuals
and the concern to preserve the civil association. The existence of a civil,
free society depends upon trust that others will keep their word without
the presence of the coercive power of the state, trust that the other values
the free association of individuals and the mutual respect that is necessary for the "give and take" of ordinary life in a free society.

Seligman uses the etiquette of smoking as an example of the way in
which agency, risk, and trust function in a free society. Before the days of
laws governing smoking, he would ask those around him if they would
mind if he smoked. If anyone objected, he would not light up. Seligman
explains that "by voluntarily refraining from smoking and so circum-
scribing my will in favor of the interests of a stranger, I was establishing,
in however passing, fleeting and inconsequential a matter, a social bond."
The act of asking permission to smoke is a recognition of the choice that
the other must make to conform or not to our wishes. We thus recognize
his agency and, in so doing, recognize his selfhood.[18]

But now there are all kinds of legal restrictions on where it is permissible to smoke. The proliferation of legal constraints eliminates both the
need and the opportunities for civility in this matter. Seligman sees the
proliferation of legal norms as inimical to the development of the trust
that is necessary for the virtue of civility. "In the absence of trust we have
'speech codes' and other forms of regulation of interpersonal behavior."[19]
The proliferation of laws and the decrease of the space where individuals
are free to choose how to act toward each other causes the downward
spiral into incivility: more laws lead to less civility, because the opportu-

nity for choice is removed, and less civility leads to more laws to compensate for the resulting uncivil conduct.

The space of the freedom of the individual to conduct himself toward others is also essential in the economic sphere of social life. Montaigne actually suggests the radical reform of the French legal system in this respect. The French, he says, are burdened with laws "which bind the people in all of their domestic affairs." He offers instead the "ingenious opinion" of Isocrates, who advised his king "to make the trades and negotiations of his subjects free, gratuitous, and lucrative" (VS117, F85). C. S. Lewis takes Montaigne as his example of "the freeborn mind." Lewis writes: "In adult life it is the man who needs, and asks, nothing of government who can criticize its acts and snap his fingers at its ideology. Read Montaigne; that's the voice of a man with his legs under his own table, eating the mutton and turnips raised on his own land. Who will talk like that when the state is everyone's schoolmaster and employer?"[20] Lewis is here especially concerned with the role of economic independence in providing an education for one's children that is not controlled by the state. Coercion erodes social virtues such as charitable giving: the more the state takes on the role of charity, the less the individual is willing and able to practice that generosity himself. Shils also makes the case that the free market helps to foster independent judgment, a fact that became obvious with the collapse of the Communist regimes of the Soviet Union and Eastern Europe. Further, the institution of private property and the autonomy of the market guarantee the autonomy of other institutions as well.

The role of individual freedom in the maintenance of a civil society is, as we saw with Montaigne, especially significant with respect to freedom of speech, because "we are men and hold together only by our word." Free speech requires the generosity, openness, and frankness that are central to his portrait of the civil character. Recall his description of the enjoyment he finds in vigorous debate, banter, and joking. Restrictions on speech in the form of "political correctness" make witty and humorous conversation impossible and destroy the opportunity for the honest exchange of opinions in which we reveal ourselves to each other and learn to trust one another. "Political correctness" is the imposition of ideological purity on speech. It is inimical to civility, because it prevents the development of the *virtue* of civility. It destroys the courage necessary to reveal oneself and to submit oneself to criticism and refutation. Civility is not a set of rules for the smooth functioning of society: it is a moral character and an ability to make moral judgments that is enjoyed by the person who possesses it. Civility includes respect for others as moral agents and respect for oneself as a moral agent who can think for himself.

Over the past few decades, we have all heard repeated calls for greater civility in our public life. At the same time, the demand for greater civility is often exposed as the mask for an attempt to silence one's opponents and to shut down free speech. Both are true. Civility has declined. And in some cases, accusing one's opponent of incivility is a way to silence him. As Bejan explains, "Designating certain behaviors or beliefs as 'uncivil' effectively banishes them beyond the pale of conversational community." Demands for "a civilizing discourse" can aim at silencing dissent and marginalizing already marginal groups.[21]

Increasingly, attempts to reconcile the practice of civility with the right of free speech lead to restrictions on speech that are supposed to protect everyone—or at least certain groups—from being offended. This is especially so on college campuses. Precisely where one might expect the greatest freedom of speech, "safe spaces" and "trigger warnings" are now the norm. As Bejan says: "Controversies about whether to tame uncivil disagreements through legislation—whether through campaign finance reform, hate speech laws, or college speech codes—are thus usually presented as a conflict between free speech, on the one hand, and the demands of diversity and inclusion, on the other."[22]

The domination of ideology leads to the control of speech because, for the ideological mind, the most important questions of human life have been settled, and no disagreement is permitted. Disagreement becomes evil and must be suppressed. "Speech codes" and the enforcement of "politically correct" speech are, however, actually inimical to civility, although these are usually defended as necessary and essential to civility. The conflict between civility and free speech cannot be resolved by any code of conduct or by any speech code. Like all clashes of "rights," the clash of my right to free speech and your right not to be offended leads to an impasse that is impossible to resolve on the level of rights. The impasse reveals our confusion over what civility is and what it is not.

In his "Civility and the Limits of the Tolerable," Edwin Delattre argues against this ethos of "political correctness." In particular, he is critical of the prevalent idea that tolerance of differences and being "non-judgmental" are the highest virtues and that judging others or their ways of thinking, feeling, and acting is itself uncivil. On the contrary, these ideas are actually destructive of the virtue of civility, because there is an essential difference between respect and nonjudgmental tolerance. Tolerance "normally presupposes judgment in the sense that we *tolerate* what we have judged to be in some way wrong, deficient, or objectionable, but not to merit our interference." The idea that being civil means being nonjudgmentally tolerant reduces civility to a "demeaning sensitivity."[23] We see this servile sensitivity in the substitution of the autobiographical revelation for the normative assertion or judgment. "The assertion that X is false or wrong demands justification, the giving of reasons, respect for evidence, knowledge of relevant fact and principles that may be adduced; and such statements lend themselves to critical consideration, objection, refutation, disconfirmation, refinement. That is, they require the exercise of judgment. . . . By contrast, the autobiographical report 'I am not comfortable with X' cannot be logically criticized." This exclusion of reason from discourse is, in effect, *uncivil*.[24]

When civility is reduced to sensitivity, indiscriminate tolerance, and disregard for truth, it can no longer be understood in relation to liberal learning, manners and morals, or the discourse of civilized people. "Indeed, where the idea of civility is equated with the idea of sensitively coddling sensitivities that makes us too frail to bear the truth, civility can no longer be associated with our having any sort of genuine and decent respect for one another. It is, after all, an expression of pity, not of respect, to say of persons that they are too sensitive, too fragile, ever to bear learning that they have made, or are making, a mistake."[25] This demeaning and servile sensitivity reduces the individual to a whimpering victim, usually a mere member of a victim group, rather than affirming the individual as an independent moral agent. Genuine respect for others means treating them as intelligent human beings who have the willingness and the strength to bear disagreement and criticism.

Montaigne tells us that he enjoys banter and joking and is "perfect in forbearance" in the give-and-take of what we would call teasing. The suffocating effects of political correctness can be seen in the disappearance of comedy, humor, and irony. Irony is hardly recognized anymore. Laughing at oneself, self-deprecating humor, is met with incomprehension. Comedy has been replaced by rage and hatred because everything has become political. But ethnic jokes, jokes about men and about women, actually foster civility. They are a way of treating differences as amusing, not serious. They allow for the healthy expression of the recognition of difference and the diffusion of tension. The affectionate banter and irony of men and women about their differences is no longer possible when everything is reduced to politics. The disappearance of comedy, humor, and irony—this deadly seriousness—is a symptom of the pervasiveness of ideological purity, an inability to accept the imperfections resulting from the freedom of social life and the loss of the capacity to forgive the unintended slights of spontaneous social interaction.

Universities and Liberal Education

The independence of the universities from politics is crucial to the maintenance of civil society. Shils argues that the universities should, in principle, be "an authority standing outside the political struggle."[26] In fact, however, there is perhaps no other institution that has become more thoroughly politicized than the university. With few exceptions, our colleges and universities have abandoned, with a vengeance, the study of the tradition and replaced it with ideological indoctrination.

The university is not the product of the eighteenth-century Enlightenment. It is rather the product of medieval culture both in terms of its internal structure of authority and in terms of its underlying theoretical principle. The medieval university was a fairly simple organization of students and masters, governed for the most part by the general assembly of the masters. Both religious and temporal authorities provided various forms of protection for the universities. "One can only marvel at the care with which both church and state respected the 'liberties' of the medieval university. No modern university enjoys the independence . . . that the University of Paris did in the Middle Ages."[27]

The independence of the university is grounded in its essential defining purpose, the pursuit of truth. The fact that the university emerged as an independent institution in the Middle Ages is a reflection of the Christian conviction that faith has nothing to fear from reason. Reason can and should pursue the truth about the world and must have the freedom to do so. Reason, rightly pursued in the arts and sciences, will not contradict the truths of faith.

The practices of academic freedom and tenure make sense only if the purpose of the university is the pursuit of truth. Current discussions of tenure and academic freedom often betray a fundamental confusion about the meaning of these practices and prerogatives. Tenure is mistakenly identified with job security; academic freedom is confused with the right of free speech enjoyed by all citizens and protected by the First Amendment.[28]

Tenure does indeed guarantee job security, and this is undeniably a great personal benefit to the individual. But job security cannot be the reason for the practice of conferring tenure. Tenure has emerged as a status in only two institutions, the academy and the judiciary. What can make sense of this? These institutions are such that their proper activities require that they be free from external and internal constraint and interference, especially from the pressures of politics. Hence, the university must be self-governing, and the faculty must have principal responsibility for the self-governance of the institution. Further, precisely because academic disciplines are *disciplines*, and so involve a kind of constraint constituted by the proper ends of those disciplines, along with their traditional practices, methods, and findings, they must in large measure be self-governing.

Tenure and academic freedom are completely unnecessary and could not have emerged in institutions devoted to career training. Career training programs are properly subject to social and economic pressures and can be run efficiently by managers supervising a group of part-time trainers. There is no question here of the pursuit of truth, as there is in the disciplines of the liberal arts and sciences.

Academic freedom is not the same as the right of free speech. Academic freedom is the freedom to pursue the truth about a given subject and the freedom to teach it to others. It makes sense only in relation to the disciplines of the liberal arts and sciences. We acknowledge the distinction between academic freedom and political freedom of speech when we acknowledge that no professor, under cover of academic freedom, has the right to use his classes for anything other than the subject matter of his discipline. Academic freedom refers to the rights of inquiry in a teacher's discipline, not to the expression of personal or political views. For example, we would not find it acceptable for a biology professor to turn his course into a Bible study or for a professor of literature to use his lectures to campaign for a political candidate. We recognize these as abuses. Similarly, we would resist any attempt to require that same biology professor to teach the Bible in his courses or that same professor of literature to endorse a political candidate in his classes.

Academic freedom and tenure exist for the sake of institutional integrity and for the integrity of the academic disciplines. That integrity is destroyed with the increasing politicization of the academy, a corruption that is evident in such policies as speech codes and the enforcement of politically correct attitudes and behavior. Current intellectual trends would have us believe that there is no such thing as truth and that "everything is political." But, if that is so, there are no grounds on which to justify the prerogatives of tenure and academic freedom that academics hold so dear. And if political considerations determine curricular and tenure decisions, then there are no grounds for asserting institutional autonomy. The study of the liberal arts, then, contributes to the practice of civility only on condition that they have not been politicized and that the university remains a free institution that stands above the political conflicts of the moment.

Defining the liberal arts in terms of the pursuit of truth and knowledge takes us back to the foundational Aristotelian distinction between activities that are ends in themselves and activities that are directed toward ends outside themselves. Josef Pieper explains: "In his commentary on Aristotle's *Metaphysics*, Aquinas gives this definition: 'Only those arts are called liberal or free which are concerned with knowledge; those which are concerned with utilitarian ends that are attained through activity, however, are called servile.' . . . The liberal arts, then, include all forms of human activity which are an end in themselves; the servile arts are those which have an end beyond themselves, and more precisely an end which consists in a utilitarian result attainable in practice, a practicable result."[29]

Pieper goes on to distinguish academic education in the true sense from professional training.

> A functionary is trained. Training is defined as being concerned with some one side or aspect of man, with regard to some special subject. Education concerns the whole man; an educated man is a man with a point of view from which he takes in the whole world. Education concerns the whole man, man *capax universi*, capable of grasping the totality of existing things. . . . The question is: whether the world, defined as the world of work, is exhaustively defined; can man develop to the full as a functionary and a 'worker' and nothing else; can a full human existence be contained within an exclusively workaday existence.[30]

This defense of the liberal arts concerns both the perfection of the individual and the good of society. The recognition of the inherent dignity of every individual that is necessary for civil society is preserved in the conviction that man in his essence is not a mere instrument to be used by the state.[31] It is that conviction that accounts for the recognition of the inherent worth of "liberal" education.

John Henry Newman expresses this same understanding of the liberal arts in *The Idea of a University*: "Liberal education, viewed in itself, is simply the cultivation of the intellect, as such, and its object is nothing more or less than intellectual excellence. Every thing has its own perfection, be it higher or lower in the scale of things, and the perfection of one is not the perfection of another."[32] The intellect must have an excellence of its own, an end of its own. "Had it not such an end, there would be no meaning in calling certain intellectual exercises 'liberal,' in contrast with 'useful,' as is commonly done."[33] Further, the cultivation of the intellect is "best for the individual himself, [and] best enables him to discharge his duties to society." Newman insists that liberal education does not detach the educated man from society. The truly educated man is not a snob. On the contrary, "he is at home in any society, he has common ground with every class."[34] The truly educated man has common ground with every class because through his education he has immersed himself more deeply in the tradition that is common to all.

The natural end of liberal education as the pursuit of truth has been replaced by a variety of purposes, chosen by the individual. Many go to college for professional training and a good job. In this respect, as Patrick Deneen argues, "liberal education is replaced with servile education."[35] Deneen explains how this change harms the exercise of our freedom as citizens of a liberal order. "The liberal arts were long understood to be the essential form of education for a free people, especially citizens who aspired to self-government." The study of the great books, which had been deemed essential for free citizens, has been replaced by what had been considered "servile education," concerned exclusively with work and money making. "Today's liberals condemn a regime that once separated freeman from serf, master from slave, citizen from servant, but even as we have ascended to the summit of moral superiority over our benighted forebears by proclaiming everyone free, we have almost exclusively adopted the educational form that was reserved for those who were deprived of freedom."[36]

Professors and college administrators, perhaps on account of some lingering realization that liberal education is supposed to be something more than job training, defend the study of the humanities (and the increasing costs of college) as fostering the ability to "think critically." In *Not for Profit: Why Democracy Needs the Humanities*, Martha Nussbaum claims that the spirit of the humanities is "critical thought" and that the ideal to be sought in the study of the humanities is "critical questioning." She explains that what critical thinking entails is "a hatred of dead and imprisoning traditions."[37] Further, the goal of our teaching of critical thinking is to make students "responsible democratic citizens" and to make them "complete citizens who can think for themselves, [and] criticize tradition."[38]

Critical thinking is "unmasking" the great books of the tradition as sources of oppression, racism, sexism, homophobia, and colonialism. Deneen says: "Under liberalism, the liberal arts are instruments of personal liberation. . . . In the humanities, liberatory movements based on claims of identity regard the past as a repository of oppression, and hence displace the legitimacy of the humanities as a source of education."[39] Describing the transformation of the humanities that began more than fifty years ago, Deneen says that faculty demonstrated their progressiveness and political correctness "by showing the backwardness of the texts; they could 'create knowledge' by showing their superiority to the authors they studied; they could display their antitraditionalism by attacking the very books that were the basis of their discipline. Philosophies that preached 'the hermeneutics of suspicion,' that aimed to expose the way texts were deeply informed by inegalitarian prejudices, . . . offered the humanities the possibility of proving themselves relevant in the terms set by the modern scientific approach. . . . Professors in the humanities showed their worth by destroying the thing they studied."[40]

Although the goal of "critical thinking" would seem to be at odds with protecting students from criticism and disagreement, the claim is often made that college must be a "safe space" in which everyone's feelings must be respected and no one should be made to feel "uncomfortable." College is the safe space in which we learn to be tolerant and "nonjudgmental." In *The Coddling of the American Mind: How Good Intentions and Bad Ideas Are Setting Up a Generation for Failure*, Greg Lukianoff and Jonathan Haidt argue that this form of protection from conflict deprives young people of the experiences that their minds need, "thereby making them more fragile, anxious, and prone to seeing themselves as victims."[41] In particular, the current obsession with "microaggressions" encourages the kind of suspicion and mistrust that makes open and honest debate impossible. "The term 'microaggressions' refers to a way of thinking about brief and commonplace indignities and slights communicated to people of color (and others). Small acts of aggression are real . . . but because the definition includes accidental and *unintentional* offenses, the word 'aggression' is misleading. . . . By encouraging students to interpret the actions of others in the least generous way possible, schools that teach students about microaggressions may be encouraging students to engage in emotional reasoning and other distortions while setting themselves up for higher levels of distrust and conflict."[42] Identity politics combined with sensitivity to "microaggression" produces a culture of self-censorship.[43] "A university devoted to the pursuit of truth," on the other hand, would "prepare its students for conflict, controversy, and argument."[44]

Peter Thiel has argued that political correctness (not income inequality, racism, or sexism) is actually the central problem in our universities and our society, because it is a form of thought control that accounts for the expanding timidity in American society. Political correctness creates pressure to conform and fosters an unwillingness to think for oneself. Intolerance of "politically incorrect" viewpoints creates college campuses "full of people who look different but think alike."[45]

Contrary to the view that college is supposed to create a "safe space" by teaching that tolerance is the highest virtue and that we must be nonjudgmental, Edwin Delattre argues that education is supposed to cultivate intellectual powers and moral sensibilities, including intellectual honesty and discrimination, and the clear awareness that the well-mannered exposure of error is neither uncivil nor intolerant. "As long as a sentimental relativism pervades our institutions, we must expect cynicism within them, and opposition to intellectual and moral seriousness, self-knowledge, and wisdom."[46]

Critical thinking, understood as the unmasking of the tradition, is supposed to make "self-creation" possible. Liberated from the constraints of inherited wisdom, the individual is free to become whatever he or she chooses. Therefore, there can be no required course of study, no "core curriculum" to place restrictions on individual choice, and nothing to challenge the comfort and self-esteem of the student. The self-created critical thinker belongs to the new elite of the educated and authentic individuals who are prepared to initiate social change.

Montaigne does not defend liberal education in the way that Aquinas and Pieper do: he does not present education as the pursuit of knowledge for its own sake and as the way in which this kind of activity is the perfection of the intellect. His view of education is of a piece with his view of the self-directed individual and the formation of that individual for life in the new liberal order. As he says in his essay on the education of children, the purpose of education is the formation of judgment, and forming the judgment is making the tradition one's own in the process of self-direction: "The bees plunder the flowers here and there, but afterward they make of them honey, which is all theirs; it is no longer thyme or marjoram. Even so with the pieces borrowed from others; [the student] will transform and blend them to make a work that is all his own, to wit, his judgment. His education, work, and study aim only at forming this" (VS152, F111). One's judgment *is* one's individuality. It is "thinking for oneself." As Newman describes this in his *Idea of a University*, judgment is "intellectual self-possession."[47]

Montaigne's view of education as the formation of judgment is intended to foster the civility that he sees as necessary for modern political and moral life. Although the goal of the formation of judgment is essentially different from the traditional ends of the pursuit of truth and the perfection of the intellect, it does seek to preserve, in some way, the fragments of the tradition. Montaigne creates his character out of the fragments of the tradition: authenticity is not just following one's desires and passions. The character that Montaigne brings into being is the character of the individual suited for life in society. Judgment is necessary for civility, which operates in the space of free choice and individuality. Contrary to Nussbaum, thinking for oneself can only be done against the background of the tradition. That is why we should study the humanities and especially the history of philosophy.

Michael Oakeshott's account of liberal education appears to be indebted to Montaigne, preserving the place of tradition but directed to modern forms of political life. As Oakeshott puts it, our inheritance—our tradition—is "the ground and context of every judgment of better and worse." Cultivating judgment requires engagement with the tradition, because, as Oakeshott says, "to see oneself reflected in the mirror of the present world is to see a sadly distorted image of a human being." The task of the teacher is to free his pupils from servitude to the present, to current dominant feelings, emotions, images, ideas, and beliefs.[48] Education is not about "the fleeting wants and sudden enthusiasms" of contemporary life. It requires direction and restraint, and so it cannot be immediately connected with the current wants or "interests" of the learner. Good judgment requires what Oakeshott calls the "discipline of inclination," which fosters the habits of attention, concentration, exactness, courage, and intellectual honesty.[49] In other words, although judgment must ultimately be exercised with respect to the choices that must be made in everyday life, it cannot be *acquired* by attention to the "burning questions of the day": it is the tradition that is the ground and context of judgment. Self-creation, without a strong grounding in the great books of the tradition, is merely about the fleeting wants and sudden enthusiasms of contemporary life. Montaigne's authenticity is built out of the classical-Christian tradition and prepares him to live among others as the man who *knows how* to belong to himself.[50]

In his essay "The Voice of Poetry in the Conversation of Mankind," Oakeshott quotes William Cory, master at Eton, in his address to his students:

> You go to a great school not so much for knowledge as for arts and habits; for the habit of attention, for the art of expression, for the art of assuming at a moment's notice, a new intellectual position, for the art of entering quickly into another person's thoughts, for the habit of submitting to censure and refutation, for the art of indicating assent or dissent in graduated terms, for the habit of regarding minute points of accuracy, for the art of working out what is possible in a given time, for taste, discrimination, for mental courage and mental soberness. Above all you go to a great school for self-knowledge.[51]

Learning to think is "learning to recognize and enjoy the intellectual virtues": disinterested curiosity, patience, intellectual honesty, exactness, industry, concentration, doubt, sensibility to small differences, the ability to recognize intellectual elegance, and the disposition to submit to refutation.[52] These intellectual virtues cannot be reduced to "critical thinking."

It is especially remarkable that, for Oakeshott, the most important achievement of liberal education with respect to judgment is "the ability to detect the individual intelligence" that is at work in every human being—that is, to detect the "style" of another human being in what he says. Style is "the choice made, not according to the rules, but within the area of freedom left by the negative operation of rules."[53] In other words, it is the way in which the individual exercises his judgment. So judgment is what constitutes individuality and, at the same time, makes possible the recognition of individuality in others. Liberal education, then, is for the sake of the individual himself, but, at the same time, it fashions him as a civil character.

As Erich Auerbach claims, Montaigne was the first author who wrote for the nonspecialized but educated reader: "By the success of the *Essays* the educated public first revealed its existence."[54] That is, Montaigne actually discovers and brings this public into existence in the modern world. As David Hume argues in his essay "Of Essay-Writing," the essay form brings together what he calls the learned and the conversible worlds. Experience, upon which philosophy rests, is to be found only "in common life and conversation."[55] And Pascal describes Montaigne's style as composed of thoughts born out of the ordinary conversations of life.

Oakeshott sees the *Essays* as the clearest example of "the conversation of mankind." This conversation, he says, "is not only the greatest but also the most hardly sustained of all the accomplishments of mankind. Men have never been wanting who have had this understanding of human activity and intercourse, but few have embraced it without reserve and without misgiving, and on this account it is proper to mention the most notable of those who have done so: Michel de Montaigne."[56] That Montaigne embraced this activity "without reserve and without misgiving" is a manifestation of his generous sociability.

The contrast between "critical thinking" and the formation of judgment can be further elucidated with respect to the study of political philosophy. If the study of political philosophy is limited to the discussion of "the burning questions of the day," it can give us little guidance about how to think about these questions. Political reasoning, according to Oakeshott, is not about ideals of perfection to be achieved in the future but about intimations of what is already present in the tradition. If we see political reasoning that way, "our mistakes of understanding will be less frequent and less disastrous," because we will escape the ideological illusion that we can remodel society according to a dream or a principle.[57] As Machiavelli puts it: "Education, by making you a better knower of the world, makes you rejoice less in the good and be less aggrieved with the bad."[58]

Liberal education helps us to cultivate "the highest and most easily destroyed of human capacities," the "negative capability" that is the ability to suspend one's judgment.[59] The study of the history of political philosophy fosters a skeptical understanding of political activity. "The more thoroughly we understand our own political tradition, the more readily its whole resources are available to us, the less likely we shall be to embrace the illusions which wait for the ignorant and the unwary: the illusion that politics can get on without a tradition of behavior."[60]

Most important, philosophy leads us to consider the place of politics within our total experience. Philosophy is not ideology or the defense of ideology. Philosophy allows us to see more clearly what is more important than politics. The virtue of civility rests on this conviction of the limits of politics and this acceptance of the imperfection of political and social life.

SIX

Living among the Ruins

The Disintegration of the Social Bond

Christian piety annihilates the human self, and human civility hides it, and suppresses it.

—Pascal, *Pensées*

If it should happen . . . that the opposition to tradition should lead to its complete rejection, we would be absolutely correct to speak of the end of the humane world.

—Leszek Kolakowski, "Von Sinn der Tradition"

The only reason we are still alive is our inconsistency in not having actually silenced all tradition. . . . We are facing the radical impossibility of a meaningful common existence, although no one can imagine what this end would be like.

—Gerhard Kruger, *Geschichte und Tradition*

The disintegration of the social bond is the moral disaster that causes us to seek the meaning, the sources, and the conditions of civility. The failure of civility shows that the preservation of civility depends upon the preservation of the "higher things," which are precisely those things that the tradition preserves but the modern liberal order suppresses. If the state crushes all of the avenues of access to what is higher than politics, or if the institutions that preserve the tradition are undermined from within, civility deteriorates and the social bond is dissolved. If the restraints of the tradition lose their hold, the strong have nothing that could limit their desires, and the weak have nothing to which they can appeal. The natural desire for mastery then reemerges but now without the constraints available in the tradition.

Civility is a human, philosophical invention. The flaw in civility is in its origin, in the philosophical act itself. As Pascal claims, human civility is the concealment and suppression, not the annihilation, of the human self. The modern philosophical act of reflection originates not in the desire for contemplative knowledge but in the desire for mastery over nature, the mastery that belongs to God alone. As Gerhard Kruger explains, the philosophical self-consciousness of reflection is defiance of divine omnipotence and of the tradition that directs and submits man to God. The ultimate outcome of the emancipation of man by man is the mastery of man by man. As Rémi Brague argues, "The domination of man over nature turns into a domination of man over man. . . . In truth, this means the domination of certain human beings over others, the domination of those who best represent the type 'man' over the others."[1]

In *The End of the Modern World*, Romano Guardini points to "a kind of dishonesty which . . . is integral to the contemporary world itself." At the beginning of the modern age, the attack on Christianity was directed against the content of revelation, not against the ethical values that had developed under the influence of faith. "At the same time modern culture claimed those very values as its own foundation. . . . The modern world dedicated itself to the theory that it had discovered and developed ethical values." Guardini argues that "those who maintain that these values and cultural attitudes are simply one with the autonomous development of human nature misunderstand the essential role of a Christian economy of Revelation, Faith and Grace." These ethical values can endure for a time, "but gradually they too will be lost."[2]

Montaigne invents the civil character out of the fragments of the classical-Christian tradition. Because his project is the reformation of mores, he must use the classical and Christian sensibilities that are already there in the tradition—namely, classical nobility and Christian charity. The tradition unites the classical and the Christian and preserves both nobility and charity.

Civility has to fail, because it originates in the act that forgets the tradition—that is, it originates in the destruction of the very conditions that make it possible: it can survive only as long as and to the extent that the tradition—the source of its elements—is kept alive. It is so fragile because the pieces of this philosophical construction have been cut off from the whole in which they have their meaning. Civility depends upon the nobility of the civil character, yet the honor that keeps nobility alive is suppressed. Civility depends upon Christian charity, yet the religious tradition is forgotten in the reordering of man to man. The suppression of honor and religion results in the disappearance of any public acknowledgment of the necessity of the higher things.

The disintegration of the social bond, then, flows primarily from two sources: the success of the attack on honor and the elimination of the public presence of religion. "The 'outdated status' of honor is what happened to honor as a result of the assault on the ethics of gentlemanly virtue mounted by modern political philosophy from its beginning. That assault [is] very near the core of modern political philosophy."[3] Civility has disappeared because honor and the idea of the gentlemen have almost disappeared and have become objects of derision and ridicule. Without honor, civility withers and dies and is noticed more by its absence than its presence.

In the preceding chapters, the disappearance of honor has been a central theme: the philosopher's renunciation of self-esteem, the revaluing of the higher and the lower things, the reduction of greatness from shining noble deeds to invisible self-possession and self-containment, and the hiddenness of nobility and greatness necessary for the suppression of natural mastery and the acceptance of unnatural equality. As I have argued in chapter 4, these are radical departures from the tradition that amount to the privatization of morality. And the privatization of morality means that there is no public standard of morality, there are no public standards of honor and shame, and therefore there is no possibility of moral community. In this chapter, I focus on the disappearance of religion from public life and the reemergence of the unbridled desire for mastery.

RELIGION IN THE PUBLIC SPHERE

Civility is about how men look at each other, how they regard each other: it must be a deeply engrained disposition to acknowledge the inherent worth of the individual. In religious terms, its source is the recognition of the image of God in every other human being. When we try to understand the failure of civility, we realize why the sacred is the source of the social bond and why religion is essential to the preservation of civility. Civility is the sum of "the pre-contractual elements of solidarity" whose source is the sacred.[4]

The social bond in a free society depends upon recognition of the individuality and freedom of each of the participants. Shils argues that our appreciation of the autonomy and intrinsic worth of the individual human being and of the value of his self-expression is fundamentally an appreciation of the sacredness of his existence. And that appreciation can come only from religious tradition.[5] In his essay "The Nature and Meaning of Sociality," Oakeshott argues that "God is the only principle of sociability which will explain the facts of life. Society becomes possible by religion."[6]

The social bond of medieval Europe was found in worship, in the celebration of the Eucharist. The loftiest theologian was at one with the least educated laborer. In that sense, there were no "elites." The highest human activity, contemplation, has its roots in the divine liturgy, in which all share and participate. As Thomas Aquinas writes: "Before the coming of Christ none of the philosophers was able, however great his effort, to know as much about God or about the means necessary for obtaining eternal life, as any old woman knows by faith since Christ came down upon earth."[7]

C. S. Lewis, recounting his own experience, gives us a concrete example of what this social bond actually means. He disliked going to church on Sundays; he disliked the hymns, which he considered to be fifth-rate poems set to sixth-rate music. "But as I went on I saw the great merit of it. I came up against different people of quite different outlooks and different education, and then gradually my conceit just began peeling off. I realized that the hymns were, nevertheless, being sung with devotion and benefit by an old saint in elastic-side boots in the opposite pew, and then you realize that you aren't fit to clean those boots."[8] Natural and conventional differences are not erased, but they become insignificant in the presence of the reality of the Incarnation. This transformation is what Pascal refers to as the annihilation of the self.

In his "Notes towards the Definition of Culture," T. S. Eliot sets out the conditions for the common culture created by sacred tradition: "While we believe that the same religion may inform a variety of cultures, we may ask whether any culture could come into being, or maintain itself, without a religious basis. We may go further and ask whether what we call the culture, and what we call the religion, of a people are not different aspects of the same thing: the culture being, essentially, the incarnation (so to speak) of the religion of a people."[9] The situation that Eliot describes is one in which "the culture of an artist or a philosopher is distinct from that of a mine worker or a field labourer; the culture of a poet will be somewhat different from that of a politician; but in a healthy society these are all parts of the same culture."[10]

The Reformation destroyed the unity of Christendom, undermining the public authority of the Church and making faith a purely private matter. Teresa Bejan describes "the profundity of the religious, social, and political rifts the Reformation instigated within Western Christendom"[11] and the way in which "the bonds of church communion [were] shattered by the Reformation."[12] She details "the threat posed to the *concordia* of Christendom by the new and highly uncivil forms of disagreement to which the Reformation gave rise . . . [and] how the ancient ideal of social harmony as *concordia* embraced by early modern Christians was fatally challenged after the Reformation by the simultaneous explosions of fundamental disagreement, partisan polemic, and conscientious incivility."[13] It is clear from Bejan's account that the concept of civility arose "in early modern attempts to refasten the social bonds severed by the Reformation."[14]

For the Catholic Church, the sources of authority are both Scripture and tradition. The Reformation rejected tradition as a source of authority. At the same time, modern philosophy established the independence of human reason from faith and from the criterion of truth that had grounded philosophy from the time of Plato through the Middle Ages.

Modern philosophy's radical break with the philosophical and theological tradition led inevitably to the eighteenth-century Enlightenment, which only brought modernity to its logical conclusion.

The history of the modern world with respect to the public status of religion is the gradual suppression of religion and the replacement of the sacred tradition by ideological politics, beginning with the subordination of religion to the state and culminating in the disappearance of religion and the politicization of the churches themselves. Salvation must come not through the mystery of Christian revelation but through an ideological politics that seeks to control, by force if necessary, every aspect of life.

Early modern philosophers in general acknowledge the usefulness of religion for the social bond. Montaigne himself does see the importance of religion and of Catholicism in particular for the maintenance of the social bond.[15] He criticizes the Protestant Reformation for its insistence on the privacy of faith: "It seems to me very iniquitous to want to subject *public and immutable institutions* and observances to the instability of a private fancy (private reason has only a private jurisdiction), and to attempt against divine laws what no government would endure against civil laws" (VS121, F88, emphasis added). He criticizes the English who, in his own lifetime, have changed several times "not only in political matters, in which people want to dispense with constancy, but in the most important subject that can be, [that is,] religion" (VS579, F436). He recognizes the need for the support of the elements of civility that come from Christianity, especially forgiveness and compassion.

But for Enlightenment philosophers of the eighteenth century, Christianity is to be replaced by a new, universal and natural religion that is purely instrumental. Voltaire, for example, saw no need for a religious foundation based on revelation in order to establish a new universal morality. Jesus Christ was a great and admirable man, but only a man. Rousseau refers to religion as "one of the great bonds" of society.[16] His "civil religion," which has no doctrines except toleration and sociability, is designed to support the "general will," not to create a community of worship of a transcendent God. Kant's *Religion within the Limits of Reason Alone*, with its elimination of every visible trace of traditional Christianity, offers no possibility of real community.

Religious sentiment and belief must remain hidden in one's heart. Christianity becomes a private matter never to appear in public life. But Christianity cannot live in the privacy of the heart: it is the religion of publicness, because it claims to be the religion of truth.[17] Because it is shared and handed down, Christian tradition is public truth, accessible to all men, regardless of education and social class. Its publicness is essential to a strong social bond. The civil religion cannot replace the tradition that permeates everyday life with the sacred.

The unifying principle and defining trait of the Enlightenment, according to Vincenzo Ferrone, is the idea of "the emancipation of man through man." The Enlightenment was an emancipation project intended to create a new civilization grounded in the autonomy of human reason and the centrality of man. First and foremost, then, the Enlightenment means emancipation from tradition, especially religious tradition, and the elimination of the transcendence of the divine in favor an "entirely immanent [human] standpoint."[18]

The Enlightenment, in turn, gave way to the realization that reason, freed from its dependence on truth, is only an instrument of domination. Nietzsche opened the way to the postmodern and post-Enlightenment era by unmasking the true face of human nature and its dominant instinct, the will to power, which had only been concealed by Enlightenment claims of the emancipation of man through reason.[19] But in its rejection of reason, postmodernism fails to recognize or acknowledge that "it is modern philosophical rationalism, the Enlightenment, not philosophy [as such], that ends in the rejection of reason. 'Reason itself' can be 'rejected by philosophy itself' because the reason that is rejected has been constituted by philosophy itself," in the modern philosophical act.[20] The emancipation of man by man, under the banner of autonomous reason, inevitably leads to the emancipation of man from reason itself.

Postmodernism abandons even the modern and Enlightenment acknowledgment that religion is an indispensable support for the social bond. According to Richard Rorty, postmodernism has brought us past the time when "we felt a need to worship something which lay beyond the visible world." We must "try to get to the point where we no longer worship *anything*, where we treat *nothing* as a quasi divinity, where we treat *everything*—our language, our conscience, our community—as a product of time and chance."[21] If we are to achieve the liberal utopia of unlimited freedom, every trace of religion must be purged: "In its ideal form, the culture of liberalism would be one which was enlightened, secular through and through. It would be one in which no trace of divinity remained."[22] The liberal utopia of unlimited freedom has replaced the salvation that comes through the Church.

It might be objected that religion is not the social bond that remains above politics but rather the cause of political conflict. No doubt the competing claims of church and state, of spiritual and temporal spheres of authority, were always a source of tension and disagreement in the Middle Ages and into the early modern period. Early modern philosophers, confronted with civil and religious conflict, thought it necessary to subject religion to the state. But the lines between church and state are difficult to draw, since both church and state are concerned with moral issues.

My point is that, in spite of the problems of conflicting spheres of authority, religion is essential to the preservation of civility. The practice of religion preserves the "higher things" in a condition in which the higher things are under constant attack. If religious tradition is the source of recognition of the intrinsic worth of the human being and if it is the sum of the precontractual elements of solidarity, then the suppression of religion and religious expression is very harmful to civility. In particular, it is destructive of civility when religious believers are told that their participation in public debates on matters such as abortion is not welcome, that it is somehow illegitimate to introduce religious considerations into public discourse. This is especially harmful when their participation is dismissed on the grounds that religious belief and rational argument are incompatible, that religious belief concerning moral matters is based solely on Scripture and cannot be rationally justified. In fact, the Catholic tradition has always maintained that faith and reason are not at odds and that Christian moral beliefs can always be explained and defended on rational grounds. To dismiss Christians and other believers in this way is to tell them that they are outside the social bond, beyond the pale of civility.[23] The demand for a thoroughly secular society is a failure to recognize that religion is the greatest support for the civil character.

Christianity is all but dead in Europe. Religion is private, the churches are empty, and the state is aggressively secular. At the same time, the Islamic population has increased dramatically. In the face of this situation, Vincenzo Ferrone dismisses the efforts of the Catholic Church to salvage what is good in the idea of the Enlightenment. The philosopher Jürgen Habermas, who argues for the viability of Enlightenment rationality, and Cardinal Joseph Ratzinger (later Pope Benedict XVI) engaged in a dialogue in which they agreed on the need for a postsecular society with religion occupying a central position. In 1996, Pope John Paul II held a three-day seminar at which eminent scholars, philosophers, and theologians discussed both the merits of the Enlightenment and the consequences of denying the role of God in history, such as the rise of totalitarianism. In the words of one of the participants, theologian Robert Spaemann, "Only religion can save the Enlightenment . . . because religion understands the Enlightenment better than the latter understands itself." But for Ferrone, the Catholic Church is "an unwanted third party" in the debate over the value of the Enlightenment.[24]

In this context, the question of the possibility of the integration of Muslims into Western society can be raised in terms of the role of Christianity in the preservation of a society that is "civil." In *Beyond Radical Secularism: How France and the Christian West Should Respond to the Islamic Challenge*, Pierre Manent describes "radical" secularism as not simply the recognition of the different spheres of authority of government and religion, but as "the neutralization of religion in society," which amounts to making religion disappear as a social and spiritual force.[25] It is almost impossible for any "enlightened" European to take religion seriously as a power able to motivate and give direction to human beings today. Therefore, Europeans understand neither their own society, which has roots in Catholic Christianity, nor the strength and religious seriousness of the Islamic community.

Manent argues that the separation of politics and religion is "not a political principle that is sufficient unto itself." Although the political order and the religious order must in some ways be distinct, if believers and nonbelievers are to be citizens of the same political body, the political and the religious must also enjoy some kind of unity.[26] "Secularism is a governmental arrangement that does not exhaust the meaning of common life, and that, moreover, provides only an abstract and quite impoverished picture of it. One does not live a separation."[27] The enlightened opinion that radical secularism, with its neutralization of religion and with its own set of "values" grounded in individual rights, is sufficient to accomplish the full integration of Muslims into the life of a nation is an empty illusion.

Manent concludes that the West must first acknowledge its own Christian origins and character before it can truly and seriously address the challenge posed by Islam. "Our Muslim fellow citizens will be able to raise the question of their relationship to the social and political whole only if the question of the whole is raised by all, and this over the whole range of the political body."[28] Because his most immediate audience is French, Manent calls specifically on Catholics to take up this challenge, but his argument is also intended for Christians throughout the Western world. "The Muslim question obligates Catholics to recover self-awareness, and to recover forgotten questions, that of their place in the political body, that of the meaning of their participation in common affairs and that of their attention to 'ultimate ends,' and of their confidence in Providence."[29]

In contrast to Ferrone, who regards the Church as an unwelcome participant in discussions of the fate of the Enlightenment, Manent says that "the Catholic Church is the only spiritual force that approaches matters in such a way as to take into account the views of others in a deliberate and as it were thematic way." In fact, "it is Catholics who most often have taken the initiative of these 'dialogues' in which one seeks, not only to facilitate coexistence between Catholics and Muslims, but also to give a positive meaning to religious plurality." In the spiritually fragmented world of Western culture, the Church "is the fixed point that is concerned to relate itself intelligently to all the other points, and to which the other points can try to relate."[30]

The Church can play the role that Manent envisions for it, it can be the "fixed point," because the Church has preserved the tradition of the harmony of faith and reason. To call Christians back to an examination of the origins and the character of the West is to invite Muslims into full participation in Western society. Christianity offers the possibility of both the satisfaction of human reason and the freedom of human beings to govern themselves. Therefore, it offers an alternative to the limitations placed on reason and freedom in Islam.

In contrast to Christianity, Islam rejects the harmony of faith and reason. The Muslim community is held together by the Qur'an, the revealed law of God. Because it is from God, it cannot be questioned, cannot be submitted to examination by reason. It is simply the will of God. In *The Closing of the Muslim Mind*, Robert Reilly explains how the identification of God's nature with will rather than with reason (*logos*) implies the impossibility of moral philosophy. If God is pure will and power, then the proper response to him is submission, not understanding.[31] "Nothing that man knows or can learn by his reason can possibly carry any moral weight concerning what he must do or not do. It also means that the 'moral' obligations that God sets upon man do not originate in reason, nor is there anything that God is obligated to do by reason. God can command what is evil to be good, or good to be evil. Reason has nothing to do with justice or morality. Only absolute divine will does."[32] This primacy of God's will has a "devastating impact on the notion of human freedom," for man's freedom is "an offense to God's omnipotence."[33]

In contrast to Christianity, Islam rejects the separation of church and state. Because Islam is a revealed law, and a law that governs every aspect of human life, there can be no separation of religion and politics. Islam is both a "religion and political regime." In Islam, "the idea according to which God could leave a region of liberty to man, wait for man's choice, and respect this choice, is thus removed."[34] Muslim scholars note the refusal of Christianity to unite the religious and the political, and they attribute this to the absence of both "holy war" and a politics that could be directly derived from Scripture. The New Testament entails "the radical exclusion of any Christian *shariah*." The distinction between religion and politics is based on Christ's teaching: Give to Caesar what is Caesar's. As Rémi Brague puts it, "The purely religious nature of what Christianity claimed to bring had as a consequence a refusal to charge the details of the rules governing inter-human relationships with the weight of the Absolute."[35]

Thomas Aquinas, in his discussion of the New Law of the Gospel, explains the area of freedom that is left to man: in addition to works of faith, there are many works that are neither required nor forbidden by the New Law. Such works "are left by the Lawgiver, Christ, to the individual, according to his responsibility for others. And so each individual is free as regards works of this kind to decide what is best for him to do or avoid doing; and each man in authority is free to make arrangements for his subjects in such matters as to what they should do or avoid doing. And so even in this respect the law of the Gospel is called the *law of freedom*."[36]

Christianity's harmonization of faith and reason makes its universality possible. Reason can break down barriers to faith, showing that what is proposed for our belief is not impossible or irrational, so that faith can be freely embraced. At the same time, the independence of religion from politics makes it possible to transmit Christianity to other cultures.[37] Because it is a universal sacred tradition, it is open to differences of culture. The Church is already a multicultural society and, arguably, the only possible multicultural society. Islam, on the other hand, understands itself as the universal religion, but it does not permit either the separation of politics and religion or the harmonization of faith and reason, and that is why it must be spread by the sword and impose itself by force.

In our own day, the threat of this force comes from what Reilly and others have termed "Islamism"—that is, Muslim totalitarian ideology. Reilly argues that the nexus between Islamism and Western totalitarian ideology is the primacy of the will. The demotion of reason at the theological level is Islamism's connection with modern secular ideology and its denigration of reason, and with the subsequent celebration of the use of force.[38] "Like twentieth-century Western ideologies, Islamism places the burden of salvation upon politics, a total politics that, only through its control of every aspect of life, can bring about their version of God's kingdom on earth."[39]

Western civilization is no longer grounded in its origin, the harmony of faith and reason. Both the supremacy of the secular state and the suppression of the public truth of faith have cut us off from our inheritance of sacred tradition. Postmodernism is the rejection of both reason and faith. Reilly reports that a war of ideas is currently taking place in Islam: there are Muslim scholars who would like to see a movement within Islam to restore the primacy of reason and develop a natural law foundation for humane, political, constitutional rule.[40] He tells the story of the late Indonesian president Wahid, who, referring with great reverence to Aristotle's *Ethics*, said: "If there had not been such a book, I would have been a fundamentalist."[41] But when Muslim students come to the West for education, they are not presented with a common set of books that we hold to be essential for any educated human being living in a free society. To the extent to which the classic works of Western civilization are studied at all, they are presented as the sources of oppression. All we can offer are Western "values," chief among them the freedom to live as one pleases. From both the moral and intellectual point of view, we offer little that might spark the desire to be integrated into the remnants of our civil society.

NEW MASTERS AND NEW SLAVES

The tradition seeks to mitigate the desire for mastery because tradition is the bond that unites the strong and the weak in the worship of what is higher than both strong and weak. The natural inequalities among men are so great that Montaigne writes: "There is more distance from a given man to a given man than from a given man to a given animal" (VS258, F189). With the destruction of the tradition, civility is the way in which these unequal men are supposed to live together in peace. In particular, it is the way in which "the great" can submit themselves to the conditions for the social bond and accept the unnatural equality produced by that submission. But, as Pascal says, human civility is not the annihilation but merely the suppression and concealment of the human self. When the tradition is forgotten, the suppressed human self reemerges, but now without the orientation to the divine that directs and limits it. Civility fails when the tradition is so thoroughly forgotten that the natural desire for mastery, unrestrained by anything higher, reasserts itself and is directed to the mastery of other merely natural men.

In his description of the failure of the modern project, Brague argues that the intention of man to be master of himself as well as of the universe eventuates in "the domination of certain human beings over others." The reflective "action on the self" will inevitably become "that of some persons on other persons, with the former being the active subjects deemed to realize the idea of the 'self' in its purest form."[42] The modern philosophical act itself—this "reflexive action" in which the philosopher is detached from the natural man—generates a new hierarchy, a new version of the master-slave conflict. The new, modern world rests not on nature but on the purely human act of the philosopher who becomes the new type of human being.

The reordering of man to man, which is supposed to produce equality, actually leads to the emergence of a new aristocracy. As Vincenzo Ferrone shows in his appraisal of the Enlightenment, the philosophers, on account of their "generic moral superiority," constituted a new elite, a new aristocracy.[43] And this new aristocracy was to be "a new ruling class of the Western world, replacing all traditional elites."[44] This new intellectual elite was determined to change the way people thought and to change the world through ideas. The Enlightenment—the project of making the world conform to its own idea, to the "dreams" of the philosophers—was "the laboratory of modernity."[45] And when reason is unmasked as the instrument of the will to power, the natural instinct of the domination of the strong over the weak is completely unleashed and exposed. Postmodernism is the scene of open conflict between the new masters and the new slaves.

Patrick Deneen provides an account of the way in which this new aristocracy emerges. "From the outset, liberalism held forth the promise of a new aristocracy composed of those who would flourish with the liberation of the individual from history, tradition, nature, and culture, and the demolition or attrition of institutional supports that were redefined as limits or obstacles to liberty. Those who are best provisioned by disposition (nature), upbringing (nurture), and happenstance to succeed in a world shorn of those institutional supports aspire to autonomy."[46] Liberalism "aims above all at the liberation of an elite whose ascent requires the disassembling of norms, intermediating institutions, and thick forms of community, a demolition that comes at the expense of these communities' settled forms of life."[47] Deneen sees the universities as the main source of this new aristocracy: "The educational system, transformed into a tool of liberalism, is also ultimately the systemic creation of a new aristocracy of the strong over the weak."[48]

The autonomy of self-creation is the morality of the "strong in themselves" who constitute the new elite of "self-ordered" souls suited to life in the new liberal order where each must seek the good in his particularity. The modern philosophical act creates an unbridgeable gap between the philosopher and the merely natural man. The replacement of moral virtue by authenticity or self-creation introduces a new hierarchy of free and slave: only the few authentic individuals attain the "higher sphere" of the good, while the inauthentic are cut off from this higher sphere and are left to make their needs their end. Without the tradition, there is nothing to bind free and slave. Without the tradition, there is no longer any public access to the higher things. The slave is "free," but he is left with only his needs.

The scene of the new conflict between masters and slaves is captured in Richard Rorty's account of the postmodern "liberal utopia," in which two ideals are pursued: the private ideal of self-creation (authenticity) and the public ideal of solidarity based on some version of compassion. Self-creation is the ability to describe oneself in one's own terms. The self-created individual creates the only part of himself that matters by constructing his own mind. "To create one's mind is to create one's own language, rather than let the length of one's mind be set by the language other human beings had left behind."[49] Asserting one's autonomy means trying to "get out from under inherited contingencies" and to make one's own contingencies.[50] This recognition of the contingency of our vocabularies and the contingency of our consciences is "the chief virtue of the members of a liberal society."[51] The tradition has become an "inherited contingent vocabulary."

Rorty's public ideal of solidarity and community rests on the idea that cruelty is the worst thing we can do. He tells us that he borrows his definition of "liberal" from Judith Shklar, who says that liberals are the people who think that cruelty is the worst thing we do, a judgment that originates with Montaigne.[52] As we have seen, Montaigne does claim that cruelty is the extreme of all vices, and although cruelty had always been considered a vice, he is the first philosopher to rank cruelty as the worst of all vices. In my view, Montaigne insists on the extreme evil of cruelty because he sees it as the greatest risk created by the success of his project. The elimination of the gentlemen is effected by the philosophical act of reflection: the philosopher rises above nature and reorders man to man himself, but, at the same time, he creates a new kind of distance between the philosopher and the natural man, not the distance between strong and weak that occurs within the natural hierarchy, but the unnatural distance between the detached judge of nature and the weak natural man. Montaigne experiences and feels this distance as pity or compassion, and he points to the Christian source of this aspect of civility, but he realizes that this distance might just as easily be experienced as contempt for the weak.

Montaigne does not explain his ranking of cruelty in terms of a common human nature, as we might expect. That he focuses so much on compassion for animals in "Of Cruelty" shows that the human species cannot be the basis of the bond of compassion. He has to establish the basis in animal nature as such, not in the human species. The detached observer can have no feeling of compassion for the natural man, for his fellow human beings, unless he has compassion for all animal life. If he is to have any bond with the weak, it must be the bond of compassion for the merely animal.

The civil wars of Montaigne's day saw incredible examples of cruelty, unsurpassed even by those recorded in the ancient histories: "We experience this every day. But that has not reconciled me to it at all. I could hardly be convinced, until I saw it, that there were souls so monstrous that they would commit murder for the mere pleasure of it . . . for the sole purpose of enjoying the pleasing spectacle of the pitiful gestures and movements, the lamentable groans and cries, of a man dying in anguish. For that is the uttermost point that cruelty can attain" (VS432, F315–16).

His focus on the *spectacle* of cruelty shows that he regards the pleasure of cruelty not as a bodily pleasure but as a kind of contemplative pleasure. Since the suffering of other men is a spectacle to the detached observer, he sees his distance from the weak as so great that he shares nothing with them and is in danger of despising the natural man. This is the great temptation of the detached observer who has risen above nature by his own power and who has no natural or religious bond with the common herd.

Rorty recognizes "the tendencies to cruelty inherent in searches for autonomy."[53] The autonomous self-creating being is Rorty's "liberal ironist." Rorty describes the liberal ironist as "the typical modern intellectual," and "the only societies which give her the freedom to articulate her alienation are liberal ones."[54] The traditional aristocracy, thoroughly engaged in the life of society, is replaced by a new "elite" that is alienated from society. As Roger Scruton observes, "When religious faith declines it becomes difficult for intellectuals to believe that they really belong to the same community as ordinary people."[55]

Rorty does not ground the judgment that cruelty is the worst thing we can do on a common human nature, because there is no such common nature. Rather, he identifies a specific kind of pain and a particular kind of cruelty that is the temptation of the liberal ironist. "Simply by being human we do not have a common bond. For all we share with all other humans is the same thing we share with all other animals—the ability to feel pain." But human beings who have been socialized in a particular language or culture "can all be given a special kind of pain. They can all be humiliated by the forcible tearing down of the particular structures of language and belief in which they were socialized."[56]

The tendency to cruelty in liberal irony is due to the fact that "ironism . . . results from awareness of the power of redescription." Redescription is unmasking, the tearing down of traditional beliefs. "But most people do not want to be redescribed. They want to be taken seriously on their own terms—taken seriously just as they are and just as they talk. The ironist tells them that the language they speak is up for grabs by her and her kind. There is potentially something very cruel about that claim. For the best way to cause people long-lasting pain is to humiliate them by making the things that seemed most important to them look futile, obsolete, and powerless."[57] The fact that Rorty identifies humiliation with cruelty shows that the ironist sees herself as superior and that the suppressed self behind the mask of civility has reemerged as the liberal elitist's contempt for and cruelty toward those who cling to the tradition.

Rorty's compassion is merely a fragment, an abstraction, from Christian belief, for he wants to preserve and foster Christian sentiments without the metaphysical underpinnings of Christian faith. We must throw away the metaphysical and religious ladders that have brought us to "the idea that reciprocal pity is a sufficient basis for political association."[58] Although "Christianity did not know that its purpose was the alleviation of cruelty, . . . we now know these things."[59] So the liberal ironist is supposed to hold fast to the sentiment of compassion, in her ironic stance, but jettison the metaphysical basis for the sentiment.

But as Nietzsche says, writing of the "slave morality" of compassion, "When one gives up Christian belief one thereby deprives oneself of the

right to Christian morality. For the latter is absolutely *not* self-evident. . . .
Christianity is a system, a consistently thought out and *complete* view of
things. If one breaks out of it a fundamental idea, the belief in God, one
thereby breaks the whole thing to pieces; one has nothing of any consequence left in one's hands."[60]

If the sacred is removed from religion, if Christianity becomes "humanism," then it can no longer be the social bond. Daniel Mahoney, in
The Idol of Our Age: How the Religion of Humanity Subverts Christianity,
writes that the religion of humanity, "woefully ignorant of sin and of the
tragic dimension of the human condition, reduces religion to a project
of this-worldly amelioration. Free-floating compassion substitutes for
charity, and a humanity conscious of its unity (and utter self-sufficiency)
puts itself in the place of the visible and invisible Church. Christians
ought to be most sensitive to what is at stake in this new and aggressive
secular religion, but today they increasingly redefine the contents of the
faith in broadly humanitarian terms. Christianity is shorn of any recog-
nizable transcendental dimension and becomes an instrument for pro-
moting egalitarian social justice."[61] The failure of civility should teach us
that the bond that unites weak and strong cannot come from humanism
and the morality of compassion. When compassion is detached from religion, the result is the reemergence of the master-slave dynamic, the
worthlessness of the individual, and the justification of extreme cruelty.
As Mahoney argues, the ethos that results from the reduction of Christian charity to compassion and sympathy is the humanitarian ethos that
is easily compatible with fevered support for abortion and euthanasia.[62]

When Christian morality is reduced to compassion and Christian
charity is reduced to social work, religion is no longer ordered to the divine, can no longer remain above politics, and can no longer serve as the
social bond. In her criticism of what she calls "popular pity," Flannery
O'Connor concludes: "When tenderness is detached from the source of
tenderness, its logical outcome is terror. It ends in forced labor camps and
in the fumes of the gas chamber."[63] When compassion is detached from
belief in the mystery of salvation, it becomes possible to inflict unspeakable cruelties on the hordes of merely natural men and women who cling
to the tradition and who resist the efforts of the elites to refashion them
in the image of the new man.

As Rémi Brague observes, "The Enlightenment passes for having been humanistic. In fact, the authors who represent it often express a disdain that borders on misanthropy toward man."[64] The destruction of the old order required the elimination of the gentlemen. For Kant, the violence and cruelty of the French Revolution, in spite of the misery produced by it and the atrocities committed in its name, "has aroused in the hearts and desires of all spectators who are not themselves caught up in it a *sympathy* which borders almost on enthusiasm. . . . It therefore cannot have been caused by anything other than a moral disposition within the human race."[65] The nature of Kant's "sympathy" shows what happens when the philosopher ceases to be a participant in the common good, when freedom is entirely separated from nature, and when reason detached from truth becomes the "dream" of an intellectual elite intent on conforming reality to its immanent standpoint. There are no longer any natural limits, and everything is possible. Reason, unrestrained by anything outside itself, leads to the terror, the absolute power of the state, and totalitarianism, for there is no effective check on human power.

Contrast the sympathy of Kant with the compassion of a Christian confronted with the suffering endured under totalitarian rule. William McGurn describes an experience he had while praying in a church in Shanghai after the death of Mao: "When China was opening up after Mao died, this columnist attended early-morning Mass at St. Ignatius Cathedral in Shanghai. The congregation was no larger than half a dozen. About three pews ahead of me was a very old Chinese woman. When she knelt, she exposed the treads on the bottoms of her sandals, revealing they'd been fashioned from old tires. A wave of pity came over me. And then I thought: I have it backwards. This woman has lived through horrendous persecution, times when all must have seemed hopeless. Yet here she was in her pew, unapologetic, unbowed and, in her own way, triumphant."[66] McGurn sees this woman as an individual, not as an unavoidable casualty on the path of progress, and he shares a sacred bond with her. Human suffering has a very different meaning within the tradition than it does within the liberal order, where "humankind has become the farthest and most authoritative horizon of human action," and "the Christian God is no longer the keystone of the sacredness of the common."[67]

The philosopher who stands in and participates in the classical-Christian tradition is an essential constituent of the common good, making the good common by remaining above the political struggle. In our postmodern world, philosophy is "unmasking," the "critical thinking" that is the destruction of tradition and the instrument of a divisive political ideology of "identity" and resentment. The implications of this for the possibility of human community are captured in the warning of Gerhard Kruger: "The only reason we are still alive is our inconsistency in not having actually silenced all tradition. . . . We are facing the radical impossibility of a meaningful common existence, although no one can imagine what this end would be like."[68]

Fragments Shored against Our Ruin

Montaigne was aware of the danger and risk of replacing the social bond of the tradition, so he offered his new civil character as the alternative to the character formed by the classical and Christian virtues. He recognized that the endurance of the social bond of civility would require certain supports, and he saw the need for the free institutions and practices, such as liberal education and religion, that would preserve the elements of the tradition necessary for that bond. However, these supports have shown themselves to be insufficient. Cut off from the integrity of the tradition and from the bond of community, they have become corrupted from within. Montaigne's project was doomed to fail because it is self-undermining. Civility—the world Montaigne made—is disintegrating as the Enlightenment's relentless advance overwhelms the traditional sources of nobility and charity that Montaigne had used to invent civility. We are now beginning to imagine what the end will be like.

Where can we turn for help in understanding our present dire condition? Are there resources within the tradition that might shed light on our way forward? Recent efforts to revive the moral philosophy of the virtues and the political philosophy of the common good and of natural law through the study of Aristotle and Aquinas are attempts to respond to the manifest absence of moral community and public standards within the structure of the liberal order. These efforts are, of course, extremely valuable in our attempts to recover the tradition and the community formed by the tradition.

In what has been described as our postmodern, post-Christian world, we can also turn to Montaigne's most profound critic, Blaise Pascal, whose fragments of an apology for the Christian religion offer us a different way into the tradition. Romano Guardini's *The End of the Modern World* originated in his attempt to explore "the meaning of Pascal's vision of man and the world." He explains: "My prolonged studies produced an intimacy with the thought of Pascal which indicates that he is related to the modern world in a manner distinctly his own, in a manner proper to one who was both a psychologist and a philosopher of the meaning of Christian existence. He belongs to that company of men who saw the whole situation of the new world which was coming to be."[69] At the center of the culture of this new world is the problem of human power in its modern sense and an ethic that would be effective for controlling the use of power. For human freedom means that man can use his power as he pleases, and within his freedom reside the possibilities of destruction and evil.[70]

Like Montaigne and virtually every modern philosopher, Pascal broke with the Aristotelian hold on metaphysics, science, and politics. He believed that the medieval Scholastic approach to nature was gravely flawed.[71] In this respect, he accepts the Cartesian break with the tradition of scientific inquiry dating back to Aristotle and carried through the Middle Ages to the Renaissance.

Like Montaigne and virtually every modern political philosopher, Pascal also breaks with the Aristotelian-Thomistic political philosophy: the common good, he says, is nothing more than a false image of charity.[72] Pascal's view of politics is indebted not to Aristotle or Aquinas but to Saint Augustine. "St. Augustine had taught that all government on earth, all power of man over man is a consequence of original sin; without the injustice of the original sin, which had destroyed the natural peace and equality among men, there would be no need for . . . the counter-injustice of human power on earth."[73] Pascal recognizes the necessity and legitimacy of the rule of men over each other, "but he is much more profoundly aware that this legitimacy is evil."[74] Pascal says that "all men naturally hate each other."[75] And "each self is the enemy of all the others and would like to tyrannize them."[76] Human civility, however, merely hides and suppresses the human self. Self-annihilation comes only through Christian piety.

Pascal rejects the Aristotelian hold on the tradition, but he also recognizes the danger of modern philosophical reflection. Guardini speaks of Pascal's awareness of the "will to domination" that motivates the "dangerous detachment" of the mind. He sees "what must happen when [reflection] detaches itself from faith and becomes autonomous; when it is placed in the service of a will to power which no longer has a light above it, nor a responsibility before God, nor a footing in grace. It then becomes an intellectual despotism suspended in nothingness and working in fortuitousness."[77]

For Pascal, Christian philosophical, theological, and moral teaching is ultimately about one question: How is the reality of our worldly experience related to the creative, infinite divine reality that is both manifested and hidden in the world of finite things?[78] In his essay on Pascal's Pensées, T. S. Eliot gives us an account of Pascal's way of answering that question. Pascal looks at the world, especially the moral world within; "he finds its character inexplicable by any non-religious theory: among religions he finds Christianity, and Catholic Christianity, to account most satisfactorily" for what he sees; "and thus, by . . . 'powerful and concurrent' reasons, he finds himself inexorably committed to the dogma of the Incarnation."[79] He begins from the reality of experience and asks how we can make sense of this experience. The only thing that can make sense of the whole of human experience is the Incarnation, uncreated and incarnate truth.

Pascal is critical of the "superficial reflection" that reduces sacred tradition to mere custom and refuses to see the essential differences between Christianity and all other religions.[80] "Tradition is the true source of truth," because it communicates and hands down not simply a set of beliefs but a reality, the entirety of the Christian mystery.[81] By finding truth in sacred tradition, Pascal shifts the center of philosophy from the human subject to Christ, who is the uncreated and incarnate Truth communicated to us in tradition.

Pascal says that "God made himself man in order to unite himself with us."[82] The Incarnation overcomes the absolute separation between divine and human: God enters time and leads a temporal life, knowing suffering and death. For Christians, God's divinity is revealed most perfectly in this abasement.[83] And nowhere is this abasement more manifest than in his death on the cross. The sign of the cross contains the whole of Christianity.[84] For Pascal, it is the cross that shows the universality of Jesus: "Thus it is for Jesus to be universal. . . . Jesus offered that [sacrifice] of the Cross for all."[85] In the end, it is not miracles, prophecies, or philosophical arguments that make people believe: "What makes them believe is the Cross."[86]

The cross, then, stands as the great contradiction to both Nietzsche's will to power and Islam's use of force. Reinhold Niebuhr says of the cross: "It is impossible to symbolize the divine goodness in history in any other way than by complete powerlessness, or rather by a consistent refusal to use power in the rivalries of history."[87] In a fragment that anticipates our own place in history, Pascal writes: "The way of God, who disposes all things with gentleness, is to instill religion into our minds with reasoned arguments and into our hearts with grace, but attempting to instill it into our hearts and minds with force and threats is to instill not religion but terror. *Terror rather than religion.*"[88] The power of Christianity is of a very different kind: "Christ did not subdue the nations by force of arms. . . . That is what makes me love him."[89]

Pascal saw with exceptional clarity the nature of human power and the limits of force. He speaks to us in the most meaningful way in our present condition: he calls us relentlessly back to the ultimate reality and meaning of the Incarnation. In the fragments of his unfinished apology, he offers us a way to understand ourselves as we are, in a world of naked power and force.

NOTES

Introduction

1. Bejan, *Mere Civility*, 10.
2. Oakeshott, *On Human Conduct*, 240–41.
3. Manent, *Montaigne*, 93–95.
4. Quint, *Montaigne and the Quality of Mercy*, 26.
5. Brague, *Kingdom of Man*, 2.
6. Ibid., 3.
7. References to the French text of the *Essais* are to Montaigne, *Les Essais*, ed. Villey and Saulnier. The English translation is Montaigne, *Complete Essays*, trans. Frame. The citation (VS539, F403) refers to p. 539 of the Villey-Saulnier edition and to p. 403 of the Frame translation.
8. Oakeshott, "Moral Life," 339.
9. See Machiavelli, *Discourses*, 111–12 (1.55.4–5).
10. Shils, *Tradition*, 185.
11. Pascal, *Pensées*, #1006.
12. Deneen, *Why Liberalism Failed*, 150.
13. Mahoney, *Idol of Our Age*, 70.
14. O'Connor, *Collected Works*, 830–31.
15. Pascal, *Pensées*, #865.

ONE. The New Adam

1. Pieper, *Tradition*, 33.
2. Congar, *Meaning of Tradition*, 10, 69.
3. Pascal, *Pensées*, #865.

4. Duffy, *Stripping of the Altars*, 265.

5. Ibid., 298.

6. Pieper, *Tradition*, 68.

7. Chadwick, *Selected Writings*, 3.

8. See Cave, *How to Read Montaigne*, 19.

9. Aristotle, *Politics* 1331a25–1331b15.

10. Aristotle, *Ethics* 1094a3–7.

11. "The active way of life is not necessarily in relation to others, as some suppose, nor those thoughts alone active that arise from activity for the sake of what results, but rather much more those that are *complete in themselves*, and the sorts of studies and thoughts that are for their own sake." Aristotle, *Politics* 1325b17–21.

12. Aristotle, *Metaphysics* 982b10–27.

13. Pieper, *Tradition*, 62–63.

14. Ibid., 35.

15. Ibid., 40–43.

16. Pieper, *Leisure*, 47, 137.

17. Aristotle, *Politics* 1281a1.

18. Ibid., 1252b30.

19. Ibid., 1332b12.

20. Pieper, *Leisure*, 41, quoting Aquinas's *Commentary on Proverbs*.

21. Slade, "Was Ist Aufklärung?," 56.

22. Pieper, *Leisure*, 67–68, and throughout.

23. Slade, "Was Ist Aufklärung?," 57.

24. Kruger, "Origin of Philosophical Self-Consciousness," 211–12.

25. Ibid.

26. Slade, "Was Ist Aufklärung?," 62–63.

27. Kruger, "Origin of Philosophical Self-Consciousness," 227–28.

28. "Whoever wants to essay himself in the same way" was included in the earlier versions but omitted in the Bordeaux Copy.

29. Manent, *Montaigne*, 21.

30. "We are all double within ourselves" (VS619, F469).

31. Manent, *Montaigne*, 110–12.

32. Slade, "Two Versions of Political Philosophy," 247.

33. Matthew 6:1–4 (Jerusalem Bible).

34. See Lefort, *Machiavelli in the Making*, 190. See also 359, for Lefort's description of the indeterminateness that Machiavelli faces in the moment of his act as the political subject.

35. There is a remarkable resemblance between what I am calling the "detached observer" and the "transcendental ego" as Gaston Berger discusses it in

The Cogito in Husserl's Philosophy. Berger says that the transcendental ego is "extraworldly" and in some sense "ineffable" (49). The transcendental ego appears more as a "gratuitous event" than anything we have accomplished deliberately (43). The transcendental ego is completely different from the soul (55), and "the subject who judges" is different from the "natural man" (18). "As soon as we lose sight of the extraworldly character of the 'I,' we fall back into nature: this is the gravest and the most constant danger to which the phenomenologist is exposed" (58). Transcendental phenomenology risks falling back into nature or vanishing in the ineffable (91).

36. Kruger, "Origin of Philosophical Self-Consciousness," 215.

37. Ibid., 231.

38. Manent, *Montaigne*, 113.

39. The intention of the "Apology for Sebond" is to bring man down to the animals, to deny that natural intelligence is unique to man. Even the ability to have the images of things in the mind without the matter, that privilege in which our soul glories, is not peculiar to man but is shared by the beasts (VS481, F354). What is unique to man is not Aristotelian intellect but freedom of imagination: "If it is true that man alone, of all the animals, has this freedom of imagination and this unruliness of thought, that represents to him that which is, that which is not, and that which he wants, the false and the true, this is an advantage that is sold him very dear and in which he has very little to glorify himself, for from it springs the principal source of the evils that press him" (VS459–60, F336). It is this freedom of imagination that allows the philosopher to rebel and free himself from nature.

40. Brague, *Kingdom of Man*, 43.

41. Bacon, *Novum Organum*, 91.

42. Ibid., 38.

43. Ibid., 7.

44. See Slade, "Rule as Sovereignty," 180. Slade discusses the way in which Machiavelli erases the distinction between theory and practice.

45. Machiavelli, *Prince*, 61 (ch. 15).

46. Manent, *Montaigne*, 161: "While the 'sages,' first of all the ancient philosophers, seeking the 'best form,' were engaged in the effort and movement of going from the received form to a better, even the best, form, Montaigne aims to install himself in *passage*." Referring to Montaigne's "plasticity," Manent describes this as "finding the form of our life in the detachment from all form" (157). See also Poulet, *Studies in Human Time*, 47: "Judgment can happen only in the very moment in which the consciousness operates. . . . In contrast to memory, judgment is accomplished entirely in a moment of actuality."

Two.   The New Order

1. Michael Oakeshott's account of philosophical reflection helps us to see what this revaluing means and how it occurs. "Philosophical reflection" is "the adventure of one who seeks to understand in other terms what he already understands and in which the understanding sought (itself inevitably conditional) is a disclosure of the *conditions* of the understanding enjoyed and not a substitute for it." Oakeshott, *On Human Conduct*, vii.

2. For examples of the way Montaigne conflates worth and value, see VS467, F342; VS633–35, F480–81; VS953, F728.

3. Brague, *Kingdom of Man*, 99–100.

4. Oakeshott, "Moral Life," 339.

5. Hobbes, *Leviathan*, 211 (pt. 1, ch. 15).

6. Oakeshott, *Politics of Faith*, 49. So also, Bouwsma, in *Waning of the Renaissance*, 226, describes this as a time of unprecedented empowerment of princes, during which the pressures of central government were felt on individuals and intermediate bodies, such as guilds and ecclesiastical organizations. The justification of such power was now a major concern of political thought.

7. Oakeshott, "Masses in Representative Democracy," 364.

8. Ibid., 365.

9. Ibid., 370.

10. Ibid., 370.

11. Ibid., 366.

12. See Slade, "Rule as Sovereignty," 179: the fundamental thesis of modern political philosophy, is that the political whole is the construct of reason. See also Slade, "Was Ist Aufklärung?," 58: "According to modern philosophy, reason as such is rule. It is the essence of reason, as modern philosophy and the Enlightenment understand reason, to rule. . . . Reason understood as rule is what makes modern philosophy *modern*."

13. Slade, "Two Versions of Political Philosophy," 243.

14. Lefort, *Machiavelli in the Making*, 199.

15. Ibid., 253–54.

16. Constant, "Liberty of the Ancients," 310.

17. Slade, "Two Versions of Political Philosophy," 252–53.

18. Hobbes, *Leviathan*, 217, 220 (pt. 2, ch. 16).

19. Ibid., 227 (pt. 2, ch. 17). See Mansfield, "Hobbes and the Science of Indirect Government," 97: "The people govern themselves through their representatives. They are not ruled directly by others, because the government has its source in themselves." Mansfield claims that the "genius of representative government," as it is described by Hobbes, is that the sovereign representative is au-

thorized to establish opinions of good and bad so that they may be removed from private judgment (108).

20. Rousseau's "general will" from which all particularity has been removed.

21. Manent, *Montaigne*, 175.

22. Manent, *Montaigne*, 177.

23. Manent, *Montaigne*, 179.

24. Oakeshott, *On Human Conduct*, 201.

25. Slade, "Two Versions of Political Philosophy," 252.

26. Hobbes, *Leviathan*, 238 (pt. 2, ch. 18).

27. Hegel, *Elements of the Philosophy of Right*, 220 (#182).

28. Slade, "Two Versions of Political Philosophy," 249.

29. Hobbes, *Leviathan*, 264 (pt. 2, ch. 21).

30. Slade, "Two Versions of Political Philosophy," 251. "Depoliticized society and decontextualized rule are the great innovations effected by modern political philosophy. It is what originally was meant by liberalism."

31. Arendt, *Human Condition*, 38.

32. Hobbes, *Leviathan*, 602 (pt. 3, ch. 42).

33. Rousseau, *On the Social Contract*, 55 (bk. 1, ch. 8).

34. Ibid., 77 (bk. 2, ch. 12).

35. Slade, "Two Versions of Political Philosophy," 250.

Three.   Authenticity

1. Aristotle, *Politics* 1337a27–30.

2. Heidegger, *Being and Time*, 78.

3. Slade, "On the Ontological Priority of Ends," 58.

4. Ibid., 61.

5. Hegel, *Elements of the Philosophy of Right*, 151 (#124).

6. Ibid., 151 (#123).

7. For a more complete discussion of Montaigne's practice of confronting the passions in their beginnings, see "Of Husbanding Your Will," especially VS1016–20, F778–80.

8. Emiliano Ferrari, in *Montaigne: Une anthropologie des passions*, sees Montaigne as a philosopher concerned with the classic questions of how to control the passions and prevent them from controlling us. He argues that Montaigne rejects the classical Greek and Stoic solution that reason must rule over the passions: rather, it is the power of the imagination that is able to produce passions to oppose and replace other passions that disturb our affective life (275). Montaigne uses diversion as a method for removing our attention from an object

of suffering and refocusing it elsewhere. Diversion thus becomes a means of dealing with the passions and enduring the human condition (259). The passions can be moderated by directing them against themselves and relating them to one another so as to compensate and temper their forces (269–70).

9. Green, *Montaigne and the Life of Freedom*, 216–17.

10. Green, "Freedom and Self-Possession," 45.

11. Green, *Montaigne and the Life of Freedom*, 216.

12. Hegel, *Elements of the Philosophy of Right*, 151 (#124).

13. Augustine, *Confessions*, 202 (10.16).

14. Hegel, *Elements of the Philosophy of Right*, 151 (#123).

15. Ibid., 220 (#182).

Four.   Civility

1. Oakeshott, *On Human Conduct*, 240–41.

2. Ibid., 237–38. See also 321.

3. In his *Montaigne: A Life*, Philippe Desan writes: "Starting in 1585, and especially after 1588, Montaigne finally succeeded in separating private life and public life. The study of Montaigne's experiments in politics nonetheless proves that this desired and stated 'very clear separation' is more a literary invention than a biographical reality" (548). It is noteworthy in this respect that Montaigne does say that he is suited to be an advisor to the prince, as in fact he was as negotiator between princes in the French civil wars. "I would have told my master home truths, and watched over his conduct, if he had been willing . . . making him see how he stands in public opinion, and opposing his flatterers. . . . I should have had enough fidelity, judgment, and independence for that. It would be a nameless office. . . . I would have this an office for one man alone. . . . And certainly I should require of that man, above all, the fidelity of silence" (1077–78, F825–26).

4. Quint, *Montaigne and the Quality of Mercy*, 20.

5. Ibid., 26.

6. Ibid., 41.

7. Ibid., 104.

8. Ibid., 107.

9. Hanson, *Soul of Battle*, 52. Hanson relies on scattered references in Xenophon, Plutarch, Pausanius, and Diodorus (52, 417).

10. Ibid., 21, 116–17.

11. Cornelius Nepos, "Epaminondas (420–362 BC)," in *Lives of Famous Men*, 86.

12. Machiavelli, *Discourses*, 55 (1.21.3).

13. Machiavelli, *Prince*, 50 (ch. 12). Epaminondas died in 362 BC. Philip became king of Macedon in 358 and occupied Thebes in 338.

14. Machiavelli, *Discourses*, 48–49 (1.17.3).

15. Ibid., 111–12 (1.55.4–5).

16. Oakeshott, *On Human Conduct*, 201.

17. Hobbes's "laws of nature" discussed in chapter 15 of *Leviathan* might well be called "the rules of civility." Hume's notion of "sympathy" as the source of the social virtues reflects this idea of loyalty. It is noteworthy that the social virtues are "agreeable in themselves," not simply useful. See Hume, *Enquiry concerning the Principles of Morals*, sec. 7.

18. Manent, *Montaigne*, 56.

19. Descartes, *Passions of the Soul*, 388 (art. 161). See Kruger, "Origin of Philosophical Self-Consciousness," 257.

20. Descartes, *Passions of the Soul*, 384 (arts. 152, 153).

21. Ibid., 384 (art. 154; emphasis added).

22. Hobbes, *Leviathan*, 207 (pt. 1, ch. 15).

23. Ibid., 220 (pt. 1, ch. 14).

24. Arendt, *Human Condition*, 236–37.

25. Ibid., 240.

26. Ibid., 238.

27. Ibid., 240–41.

28. Aristotle, *Ethics* 1123a35–1124a35.

29. Manent, *Montaigne*, 93–95.

30. Ibid., 49.

31. Seligman, "Trust, Confidence, and the Problem of Civility," 68–69. Douglas I. Thompson, *Montaigne and the Tolerance of Politics*, argues that trust is also instilled through the practice of toleration and that toleration is fostered by self-revelation. Thompson discusses how Montaigne encourages people to speak frankly and openly about themselves. By speaking openly about his deeply held convictions, even ones he cannot fully justify, Montaigne attempts to eliminate the passion with which he maintains these convictions and thereby enable more measured engagement with opposing ideas. This has implications for both ordinary conversation and formal political negotiations. Regarding all of these examples, Thompson writes: "Together, these skills and dispositions make up a set of 'negotiating capacities' that Montaigne models, broadcasts, and recommends to his reading public, to help them build a higher tolerance for contact and constructive dialogue with people on the 'other side' of the conflict in France" (158).

32. Manent, *Montaigne*, 59.

33. Pascal, *Pensées*, #745.

34. Aristotle, *Ethics* 1176b15. See also Aristotle, *Politics* 1338a10–1338b5, on leisure and "noble things."

FIVE.   The Deterioration of Civility

1. Shils, *Virtue of Civility*, 61.
2. Scruton, *Political Philosophy*, 147.
3. Shils, *Virtue of Civility*, 74.
4. Shils, *Tradition*, 185.
5. Ibid., 287.
6. Rorty, *Philosophy and the Mirror of Nature*, 333–36.
7. Rorty, *Contingency*, xvi.
8. Shils, *Virtue of Civility*, 26–27.
9. Ibid., 69–70.
10. Oakeshott, *Voice of Liberal Learning*, 164–72.
11. Ibid., 176.
12. Shils, *Tradition*, 33.
13. Shils, *Virtue of Civility*, 51.
14. Ibid., 118.
15. Bejan, *Mere Civility*, 7.
16. Shils, *Virtue of Civility*, 346.
17. Bejan, *Mere Civility*, 9.
18. Seligman, "Trust, Confidence, and the Problem of Civility," 70.
19. Ibid., 74.
20. Lewis, *God in the Dock*, 314.
21. Bejan, *Mere Civility*, 9.
22. Ibid., 7.
23. Delattre, "Civility and the Limits of the Tolerable," 154–55.
24. Ibid., 163.
25. Ibid., 164–65.
26. Shils, *Virtue of Civility*, 87.
27. Dahmus, *History of Medieval Civilization*, 567.
28. These observations on tenure and academic freedom were formulated (in unpublished documents) by my colleagues at St. Francis College: Joseph Carpino, Gerald Galgan, Nino Langiulli, and Francis Slade.
29. Pieper, *Leisure*, 37–38, quoting Aquinas, *Commentary on the Metaphysics*, 1.3.
30. Ibid., 39.

31. Ibid., 41.

32. Newman, *Idea of a University*, 92.

33. Ibid., 95.

34. Ibid., 135.

35. Deneen, *Why Liberalism Failed*, 111.

36. Ibid., 13.

37. Nussbaum, *Not for Profit*, 68.

38. Ibid., 2.

39. Deneen, *Why Liberalism Failed*, 111.

40. Ibid., 121.

41. Lukianoff and Haidt, *Coddling of the American Mind*, 32.

42. Ibid., 51.

43. Ibid., 77.

44. Ibid., 258.

45. Peter Thiel, "Competition Myth," 10–11.

46. Delattre, "Civility and the Limits of the Tolerable," 167.

47. Newman, *Idea of a University*, 115.

48. Oakeshott, *Voice of Liberal Learning*, 42–43.

49. Ibid., 68–69.

50. Andrew Delbanco's discussion of what college should do for the student avoids the reduction of liberal education to "critical thinking" and is, in some respects, in harmony with Oakeshott's. Delbanco's list of the qualities to be fostered includes "a skeptical discontent with the present, informed by a sense of the past," and "a willingness to imagine experience from perspectives other than one's own." Delbanco, *College*, 3, 32, 99–101, 134.

51. William Cory, master at Eton, quoted in Oakeshott, "Voice of Poetry," 491–92.

52. Oakeshott, *Voice of Liberal Learning*, 59.

53. Ibid.

54. Auerbach, "L'humaine condition," 308.

55. Hume, *Essays: Moral, Political, and Literary*, 534–35.

56. Oakeshott, "Voice of Poetry," 491.

57. Oakeshott, *Voice of Liberal Learning*, 174–75.

58. Machiavelli, *Discourses*, 283 (bk. 3, ch. 31).

59. Oakeshott, *Voice of Liberal Learning*, 148. The phrase "negative capability" was coined by the poet John Keats in a letter to his brothers, George and Thomas Keats. See, e.g., "[On Negative Capability: Letter to George and Tom Keats, 21, ?27 December 1817]," under "Selections from Keats's Letters," Poetry Foundation, https://www.poetryfoundation.org/articles/69384/selections-from-keatss-letters.

60. Oakeshott, *Voice of Liberal Learning*, 184.

Six.   Living among the Ruins

1. Brague, *Kingdom of Man*, 162–63.
2. Guardini, *End of the Modern World*, 120–21.
3. Slade, "Rule and Argument in Political Philosophy," 155.
4. Seligman, "Trust, Confidence, and the Problem of Civility," 68.
5. Shils, *Virtue of Civility*, 110.
6. Oakeshott, *Religion, Politics and the Moral Life*, 59–60.
7. Aquinas, *Commentary on the Apostles' Creed*, 4.
8. Lewis, *God in the Dock*, 61–62.
9. Eliot, *Christianity and Culture*, 101.
10. Ibid., 198.
11. Bejan, *Mere Civility*, 17.
12. Ibid., 139.
13. Ibid., 22.
14. Ibid., 10.
15. In *Montaigne: A Life*, Philippe Desan provides a detailed and comprehensive account of Montaigne's attitude toward La Boétie's *Memorandum* that offered recommendations for resolving the conflict between Catholics and Protestants without going so far as actually tolerating the public practice of Protestants. Montaigne agreed with his friend: "Like LaBoetie, he was opposed to any kind of religious tolerance, because he had a hard time understanding how two religions could coexist in the same country" (131). See also Desan, *Montaigne: Penser le social*. Desan claims that Montaigne considers religion to be an inherited custom and an obligation determined by tradition, rather than a choice. According to Desan, this view of religion (as something determined by tradition) is driven by political considerations as well: the good functioning of society requires immutable truths and thus a stable morality that must not be called into question by new beliefs (69). Montaigne's conservatism is not so much a philosophical stance as a "conservatism of circumstance" occasioned by the tumultuous times (71).
16. Rousseau, *On the Social Contract*, 128 (bk. 4, ch. 8).
17. Slade, "Was Ist Aufklärung?," 52.
18. Ferrone, *Enlightenment*, 14.
19. Ibid., 26.
20. Slade, "Was Ist Aufklärung?," 63.
21. Rorty, *Contingency*, 22.
22. Ibid., 45.
23. See Slade's discussion of Rorty's dismissal of those who believe as Ignatius of Loyola: "Was Ist Aufklärung?," 49–50.

24. Ferrone, *Enlightenment*, 47–52.
25. Manent, *Beyond Radical Secularism*, 27.
26. Ibid., 62.
27. Ibid., 100.
28. Ibid., 79.
29. Ibid., 102.
30. Ibid., 103–5.
31. Reilly, *Closing of the Muslim Mind*, 48.
32. Ibid., 69.
33. Ibid., 83.
34. Brague, *Eccentric Culture*, 119.
35. Ibid., 157–59.
36. Aquinas, *Summa Theologica* I-II.108.1 (in *Treatise on Law*).
37. Brague, *Eccentric Culture*, 161–62.
38. Reilly, *Closing of the Muslim Mind*, 179.
39. Ibid., 182.
40. Ibid., 193.
41. Ibid., 201.
42. Brague, *Kingdom of Man*, 160.
43. Ferrone, *Enlightenment*, 151.
44. Ibid., 92.
45. Ibid., 77.
46. Deneen, *Why Liberalism Failed*, 150.
47. Ibid., 143.
48. Ibid., 134.
49. Rorty, *Contingency*, 27.
50. Ibid., 97.
51. Ibid., 46.
52. Rorty, *Contingency*, xv, referring to Shklar, *Ordinary Vices*, 43–44.
53. Rorty, *Contingency*, 144.
54. Ibid., 89.
55. Scruton, *Political Philosophy*, 112.
56. Rorty, *Contingency*, 177.
57. Ibid., 89.
58. Ibid., 184.
59. Ibid., 55.
60. Nietzsche, *Twilight of the Idols; Anti-Christ*, 79–80.
61. Mahoney, *Idol of Our Age*, 13.
62. Ibid., 70.
63. O'Connor, *Collected Works*, 830–31.
64. Brague, *Kingdom of Man*, 156.

65. Kant, "Contest of the Faculties," 182.

66. McGurn, "China's Worst Western Import."

67. Mahoney, *Idol of Our Age*, foreword by Pierre Manent, xii.

68. Gerhard Kruger, *Geschichte und Tradition*, 28, quoted in Pieper, *Tradition*, 67–68.

69. Guardini, *End of the Modern World*, 14.

70. Ibid., 109–11.

71. McCarthy, "Pascal on Certainty and Utility," 98.

72. Pascal, *Pensées*, #210.

73. Auerbach, "On the Political Theory of Pascal," 127.

74. Ibid., 127.

75. Pascal, *Pensées*, #210.

76. Ibid., #597.

77. Guardini, *Pascal for Our Time*, 100.

78. Kolakowski, *God Owes Us Nothing*, 182.

79. Eliot, "The *Pensées* of Pascal," 360.

80. Pascal, *Pensées*, #150.

81. Congar, *Meaning of Tradition*, 13, 104, 135.

82. Pascal, *Pensées*, #381.

83. Brague, *Eccentric Culture*, 163.

84. Congar, *Meaning of Tradition*, 74.

85. Pascal, *Pensées*, #221.

86. Ibid., #842.

87. Niebuhr, *Nature and Destiny of Man*, 2:72.

88. Pascal, *Pensées*, #172.

89. Ibid., #593.

BIBLIOGRAPHY

Aquinas, Thomas. *Commentary on the Apostles' Creed*. In *The Three Greatest Prayers*, 3–98. Manchester, NH: Sophia Institute Press, 1990.

———. *Summa Theologica*. Translated by the Fathers of the English Dominican Province. 5 vols. Reprint. Notre Dame, IN: Ave Maria, 1981.

Arendt, Hannah. *The Human Condition*. Chicago: University of Chicago Press, 1958.

Aristotle. *Metaphysics*. Translated by Hippocrates G. Apostle. Bloomington: Indiana University Press, 1966.

———. *Nicomachean Ethics*. Translated by Robert C. Bartlett and Susan D. Collins. Chicago: University of Chicago Press, 2011.

———. *Politics*. Translated by Carnes Lord. Chicago: University of Chicago Press, 2013.

Auerbach, Erich. "L'humaine condition." In *Mimesis: The Representation of Reality in Western Literature*, translated by Willard R. Trask, 285–311. Princeton: Princeton University Press, 1953.

———. "On the Political Theory of Pascal." In *Scenes from the Drama of European Literature: Six Essays*, translated by Ralph Manheim, 101–29. New York: Meridian Books, 1959.

Augustine. *Confessions*. Translated by F. J. Sheed. Indianapolis: Hackett, 2006.

Bacon, Francis. *Novum Organum*. Translated by Peter Urbach and John Gibson. Chicago: Open Court, 1994.

Bejan, Teresa M. *Mere Civility: Disagreement and the Limits of Toleration*. Cambridge, MA: Harvard University Press, 2017.

Berger, Gaston. *The Cogito in Husserl's Philosophy*. Translated by Kathleen McLaughlin. Evanston, IL: Northwestern University Press, 1972.

Bouwsma, William J. *The Waning of the Renaissance, 1550–1640*. New Haven: Yale University Press, 2000.

Brague, Remi. *Eccentric Culture: A Theory of Western Civilization.* Translated by Samuel Lester. South Bend, IN: St. Augustine's Press, 2002.

———. *The Kingdom of Man: Genesis and Failure of the Modern Project.* Translated by Paul Seaton. Notre Dame, IN: University of Notre Dame Press, 2018.

Cave, Terence. *How to Read Montaigne.* London: Granta Books, 2007.

Chadwick, Henry. *Selected Writings.* Edited by William G. Rusch. Grand Rapids, MI: Eerdmans, 2017.

Congar, Yves. *The Meaning of Tradition.* Translated by A. N. Woodrow. San Francisco: Ignatius Press, 2004.

Constant, Benjamin. "The Liberty of the Ancients Compared with That of the Moderns." In *Political Writings*, edited and translated by Biancamaria Fontana, 309–28. Cambridge: Cambridge University Press, 1988.

Dahmus, Joseph Henry. *A History of Medieval Civilization.* New York: Odyssey Press, 1964.

Delattre, Edwin J. "Civility and the Limits of the Tolerable." In *Civility*, edited by Leroy S. Rouner, 151–57. Notre Dame, IN: University of Notre Dame Press, 2000.

Delbanco, Andrew. *College: What It Was, Is, and Should Be.* Princeton: Princeton University Press, 2012.

Deneen, Patrick J. *Why Liberalism Failed.* New Haven: Yale University Press, 2018.

Desan, Philippe. *Montaigne: A Life.* Translated by Steven Rendall and Lisa Neal. Princeton: Princeton University Press, 2017.

———. *Montaigne: Penser le social.* Paris: Odile Jacob, 2018.

Descartes, René. *Passions of the Soul.* In *The Philosophical Writings of Descartes*, translated by John Cottingham, Robert Stoothoff, and Dugald Murdoch, 3 vols., 1:325–404. Cambridge: Cambridge University Press, 1985–91.

Duffy, Eamon. *The Stripping of the Altars: Traditional Religion in England, 1400–1580.* New Haven: Yale University Press, 1992.

Eliot, T. S. *Christianity and Culture: The Idea of a Christian Society and Notes towards the Definition of Culture.* New York: Harcourt, Brace and World, 1949.

———. "The *Pensées* of Pascal." In *Selected Essays*, 355–68. New York: Harcourt Brace, 1932.

Ferrari, Emiliano. *Montaigne: Une anthropologie des passions.* Essais philosophiques sur Montaigne et son temps 4. Paris: Classiques Garnier, 2014.

Ferrone, Vincenzo. *The Enlightenment: History of an Idea.* Translated by Elisabetta Tarantino. Princeton: Princeton University Press, 2015.

Green, Felicity. "Freedom and Self-Possession: The Case of Montaigne's *Essais*." In *Freedom and the Construction of Europe*, edited by Quentin Skinner and Martin Van Gelderen, 2:27–45. Cambridge: Cambridge University Press, 2013.

———. *Montaigne and the Life of Freedom.* Cambridge: Cambridge University Press, 2012.

Guardini, Romano. *The End of the Modern World.* Edited by Frederick D. Wilhelmsen. Translated by Joseph Theman and Herbert Burke. Eastford, CT: Martino Fine Books, 2019. First published 1956 by Sheed and Ward (New York).

———. *Pascal for Our Time.* Translated by Brian Thompson. New York: Herder and Herder, 1966.

Hanson, Victor Davis. *The Soul of Battle: From Ancient Times to the Present Day, How Three Great Liberators Vanquished Tyranny.* New York: Free Press, 1999.

Hegel, G. W. F. *Elements of the Philosophy of Right.* Edited by Allen W. Wood. Translated by H. B. Nisbet. Cambridge: Cambridge University Press, 1991.

Heidegger, Martin. *Being and Time.* Translated by John Macquarrie and Edward Robinson. New York: Harper and Row, 1962.

Hobbes, Thomas. *Leviathan.* Edited by C. B. Macpherson. Reprint. London: Penguin Books, 1968.

Hume, David. *An Enquiry concerning the Principles of Morals.* Indianapolis: Hackett, 1983.

———. *Essays: Moral, Political, and Literary.* Edited by Eugene F. Miller. Indianapolis: Liberty Classics, 1985.

Kant, Immanuel. "Contest of the Faculties." In *Kant's Political Writings,* edited by Hans Reiss, 177–90. Cambridge: Cambridge University Press, 1970.

Kolakowski, Leszek. *God Owes Us Nothing: A Brief Remark on Pascal's Religion and on the Spirit of Jansenism.* Chicago: University of Chicago Press, 1995.

———. "Von Sinn der Tradition." *Merkur* 23, no. 12 (1969): 1086–92.

Kruger, Gerhard. *Geschichte und Tradition.* Stuttgart: Kreuz Verlag, 1948.

———. "The Origin of Philosophical Self-Consciousness." Translated by Fabrice Paradis Beland. *New Yearbook for Phenomenology and Phenomenological Philosophy* 7 (2007): 209–59. First published in *Logos* 22 (1933): 225–72.

Lefort, Claude. *Machiavelli in the Making.* Translated by Michael B. Smith. Evanston, IL: Northwestern University Press, 2012.

Lewis, C. S. *God in the Dock: Essays on Theology and Ethics.* Edited by Walter Hooper. Grand Rapids, MI: Eerdmans, 1970.

Lukianoff, Greg, and Jonathan Haidt. *The Coddling of the American Mind: How Good Intentions and Bad Ideas Are Setting Up a Generation for Failure.* New York: Penguin, 2018.

Machiavelli, Niccolò. *Discourses on Livy.* Translated by Harvey C. Mansfield and Nathan Tarcov. Chicago: University of Chicago Press, 1996.

———. *The Prince.* Translated by Harvey C. Mansfield Jr. Chicago: University of Chicago Press, 1985.

Mahoney, Daniel J. *The Idol of Our Age: How the Religion of Humanity Subverts Christianity.* New York: Encounter Books, 2018.

Manent, Pierre. *Beyond Radical Secularism: How France and the Christian West Should Respond to the Islamic Challenge.* Translated by Ralph C. Hancock. South Bend, IN: St. Augustine's Press, 2016.

———. *Montaigne: Life without Law.* Translated by Paul Seaton. Notre Dame, IN: University of Notre Dame Press, 2020.

Mansfield, Harvey. "Hobbes and the Science of Indirect Government." *American Political Science Review* 65, no. 1 (March 1971): 97–110.

McCarthy, John. "Pascal on Certainty and Utility." In *Modern Enlightenment and the Rule of Reason,* edited by John C. McCarthy, 92–123. Washington DC: Catholic University of America Press, 1998.

McGurn, William. "China's Worst Western Import." *Wall Street Journal,* September 25, 2018.

Montaigne. *The Complete Essays of Montaigne.* Translated by Donald Frame. Stanford, CA: Stanford University Press, 1943.

———. *Les Essais.* Edited by Pierre Villey and V.-L. Saulnier. 2nd ed. 3 vols. Paris: Presses Universitaires de France, 1992.

Nepos, Cornelius. *Lives of Famous Men.* Translated by Gareth Schmeling. N.p.: Coronado Press, 1971.

Newman, John Henry. *The Idea of a University.* Notre Dame, IN: University of Notre Dame Press, 1982.

Niebuhr, Reinhold. *The Nature and Destiny of Man.* Vol. 2. New York: Charles Scribner's Sons, 1964.

Nietzsche, Friedrich. *Twilight of the Idols; Anti-Christ.* Translated by R. J. Hollingdale. London: Penguin, 1968.

Nussbaum, Martha. *Not for Profit: Why Democracy Needs the Humanities.* Princeton: Princeton University Press, 2010.

Oakeshott, Michael. "The Masses in Representative Democracy." In *Rationalism in Politics and Other Essays,* 363–83.

———. "The Moral Life in the Writings of Thomas Hobbes." In *Rationalism in Politics, and Other Essays,* 295–350.

———. *On Human Conduct.* Oxford: Clarendon, 1991.

———. *The Politics of Faith and the Politics of Scepticism.* Edited by Timothy Fuller. New Haven: Yale University Press, 1996.

———. *Rationalism in Politics, and Other Essays.* Edited by Timothy Fuller. London: Methuen, 1962. Reprint, Indianapolis: Liberty Press, 1991.

———. *Religion, Politics and the Moral Life.* Edited by Timothy Fuller. New Haven: Yale University Press, 1993.

———. *The Voice of Liberal Learning.* Edited by Timothy Fuller. New Haven: Yale University Press, 1989. Reprint, Indianapolis: Liberty Fund, 2001.

———. "The Voice of Poetry in the Conversation of Mankind." In *Rationalism in Politics,* 488–541.

O'Connor, Flannery. *Collected Works*. Edited by Sally Fitzgerald. New York: Literary Classics of the United States, 1988.

Pascal, Blaise. *Pensées sur la religion*. Edited by Louis Lafuma. 3 vols. Paris: Editions du Luxembourg, 1951.

Pieper, Josef. *Leisure the Basis of Culture*. Translated by Alexander Dru. San Francisco: Ignatius Press, 2009. First published 1952 by Pantheon Books (New York).

———. *Tradition: Concept and Claim*. Translated by E. Christian Kopff. Wilmington, DE: ISI Books, 2008.

Poulet, Georges. *Studies in Human Time*. Translated by Elliott Coleman. Baltimore: Johns Hopkins University Press, 1956.

Quint, David. *Montaigne and the Quality of Mercy: Ethical and Political Themes in the Essays*. Princeton: Princeton University Press, 1998.

Reilly, Robert R. *The Closing of the Muslim Mind: How Intellectual Suicide Created the Modern Islamist Crisis*. Wilmington, DE: ISI Books, 2010.

Rorty, Richard. *Contingency, Irony, and Solidarity*. Cambridge: Cambridge University Press, 1989.

———. *Philosophy and the Mirror of Nature*. Princeton: Princeton University Press, 1971.

Rousseau, Jean-Jacques. *On the Social Contract*. Edited by Roger D. Masters. Translated by Judith R. Masters. New York: St. Martin's Press, 1978.

Scruton, Roger. *A Political Philosophy*. London: Continuum, 2006.

Seligman, Adam B. "Trust, Confidence, and the Problem of Civility." In *Civility*, edited by Leroy S. Rouner, 65–77. Notre Dame, IN: University of Notre Dame Press, 2000.

Shils, Edward. *Tradition*. Chicago: University of Chicago Press, 1981.

———. *The Virtue of Civility*. Edited by Steven Grosby. Indianapolis: Liberty Fund, 1997.

Shklar, Judith. *Ordinary Vices*. Cambridge, MA: Harvard University Press, 1984.

Slade, Francis. "On the Ontological Priority of Ends and Its Relevance to the Narrative Arts." In *Beauty, Art, and the Polis*, edited by Alice Ramos, 58–69. Washington, DC: American Maritain Association/Catholic University of America Press, 2000.

———. "Rule and Argument in Political Philosophy." In *Ethics and Theological Disclosures: The Thought of Robert Sokolowski*, edited by Guy Mansini, O.S.B., and James G. Hart, 149–61. Washington, DC: Catholic University of America Press, 2003.

———. "Rule as Sovereignty: The Universal and Homogeneous State." In *The Truthful and the Good: Essays in Honor of Robert Sokolowski*, edited by John J. Drummond and James G. Hart, 159–80. Dordrecht: Kluwer Academic, 1996.

———. "Two Versions of Political Philosophy: Teleology and the Conceptual Genesis of the Modern State." In *Natural Moral Law in Contemporary Society*, edited by Holger Zaborowski, 235–63. Washington, DC: Catholic University of America Press, 2010.

———. "Was Ist Aufklärung? Notes on Maritain, Rorty, and Bloom with Thanks but No Apologies to Immanuel Kant." In *The Common Things: Essays on Thomism and Education*, edited by Daniel McInerny, 48–68. N.p.: American Maritain Association, 1999.

Thiel, Peter. "The Competition Myth." *Intercollegiate Review*, Spring 2015, 8–11.

Thompson, Douglas I. *Montaigne and the Tolerance of Politics*. New York: Oxford University Press, 2018.

INDEX

absolute power, 62
academic freedom, 119–20
actions: ending in themselves, 18–19, 154n11; without natural constraint, 45; noble vs. servile, 21; for their own sake, 93
ambition, 77, 91
anger, 77
Arendt, Hannah, 63, 102; *The Human Condition*, 101
aristocracy, 144. *See also* new aristocracy
Aristotle: on citizenship, 67; on common good, 22; critique of, 5; description of the best city, 18, 22; *Ethics*, 18, 103; on good life, 18; on habituation to virtue, 78; on happiness, 69; on human nature, 68–69; influence of, 6, 15, 17; on judgment, 43; *Metaphysics*, 19, 22, 120; on passions, 77; philosophy of, 18, 19–20, 21, 38, 148, 149; *Politics*, 24, 63; on reason, 19; on slavery, 24
astonishment, 36, 37
Auerbach, Erich, 126
Augustine, of Hippo, Saint, 21, 84, 149

authentic individual, 8, 85
authenticity, 8; definition of, 67–68, 80; as human completeness, 70, 71, 125; inauthenticity and, 85–86; perfect, 83; as replacement of traditional ethics, 80; as self-revelation, 82–83; subjection to the compulsion of passions, 82
authentic self-possession, 71–72, 74–75, 79

Bacon, Francis, 40
becoming, 83–84
Bejan, Teresa, 2, 114, 116, 133; *Mere Civility*, 113
Berger, Gaston, 154n35
Boétie, Étienne de la, 162n15
Bouwsma, William J.: *Waning of the Renaissance*, 156n6
Brague, Rémi, 13, 48, 130, 139, 141, 147; *The Kingdom of Man*, 5

Caesar, Julius, 54
Catholicism, 133, 134, 137, 138
Cato, Marcus Porcius, 80
Christian charity, 4, 9, 13, 146

tradition: vs. civility, 9; definition of,
6; departure from, 2, 5–6, 17, 23,
27–28, 89, 131; foundation of, 6;
vs. ideology, 11, 111, 112–13; philosophy and, 20; recovery of,
148–49; reduced to custom, 28;
vs. sacred tradition, 20; as social
bond, 2, 4, 16, 113; as source of
truth, 14, 16, 21
training the disposition, 76, 78
transcendental ego, 146, 154n35
true nobility, 94
trust, 105, 159n31

universities: as guardians of tradition,
111; integrity of, 120; origin of,
118; political correctness at,
123–24; purpose of, 119; as safe
space, 123, 124; self-governance
of, 118–19. *See also* liberal
education

unlearning evil, 76, 78, 93
unnatural equality, 10

value, 48
vengeance, 77–78, 102
vice, 50, 77, 78, 93–94, 143
virtue: accidental origin of, 74–75;
civility and, 3–4; "ease" of, 3,
75–76; as noble action, 21; ranking of, 50; as social bond, 65;
strength and, 75; theological
and moral, 23
Voltaire, 12, 134

Western values, 138, 140–41
will to power, 135, 142, 150, 151
wonder, 36
work, hierarchy of leisure and, 17–18

ANN HARTLE is professor emeritus of philosophy at Emory University. She is the author of numerous books, including *Montaigne and the Origins of Modern Philosophy* and *Michel de Montaigne: Accidental Philosopher.*